A GUIDE TO HAPPY COURTSHIP AND LASTING MARRIAGE

Avoiding obvious *pitfalls* and *mistakes* in a relationship
from the beginning will ensure you and your partner
enjoy your lives thereafter.
You should know *what to look out for.*

by

Albert C. Onochie

RoseDog 🐾 Books

PITTSBURGH, PENNSYLVANIA 15222

For information or to order additional books, please write:
RoseDog Books
701 Smithfield Street, Third Floor
Pittsburgh, Pennsylvania 15222
U.S.A.
1-800-834-1803

Or visit our website and online catalogue at www.rosedogbookstore.com

TABLE OF CONTENTS

PREFACE

Marriage, the union of man and woman, is as old as humanity itself. It is an institution created by Almighty God to enable men and women "increase and multiply" and thus perpetuate the human race. Lower animals, of course, do not marry formally, but some males and females have been observed to stay faithfully together through life. Some of these lower animals have also been observed to mourn their departed "partners" in various ways through refusal to eat, refusal to leave the spots where their partners died, and even refusal to look for new partners. Both lower animals and plants, like human beings, have this wonderful gift of perpetuating themselves as designed by God and nature.

This book <u>A Guide to Happy Courtship and Lasting Marriage</u> is therefore for the serious minded man or woman, boy or girl, who intends to take marriage seriously, beginning with a purposeful and successful courtship or dating, which should culminate in a long and successful union called marriage. This book, which has been written against the backdrop of the experiences of some successful couples and interviews with them, encourages the observance or practice of religious and traditional values or virtues that help couples have lasting relationships. It is full of advice on various practical aspects of dating or courtship, marriage, and living together. It is hoped that all the alluring topics will be of interest to readers, taking one chapter at a time and trying to absorb the contents in a thoughtful or positive way.

Merely reading it through does not guarantee a successful courtship or marriage. Success depends a lot on the *interplay* of all important factors, variables and circumstances in the lives of couples. But it will definitely help readers in a very significant way to avoid *obvious pitfalls or mistakes* that usually shake foundations of courtships and marriages. It may not lead readers to "heaven" but it surely will save them from "hell," to paraphrase Sir Winston Churchill in his description of the United Nations at the formative stages. "Hell" aptly describes the sad and unfortunate situations of many couples and their relationships. These were people who professed to love each other until death but had hardly gone halfway when their marriages packed up and became history.

Courtship and marriage take various forms throughout the world. They usually follow customary practices, religious inclinations, civil laws in force and social norms. Thus, each culture, religion, government, and social group from Asia, Europe, and North America to Africa, Latin America, and Australia have different views about marriage. Some emphasize entertainment, others the spiritual side and/or the security of the partners.

Each marriage is unique. In other words, no two marriages are exactly alike as couples are different, live in different environments, have been brought up under different conditions, have varying income levels, belong to different political or social organizations, have different physical and other characteristics, etc. How couples live will certainly vary from one marriage to another, but in the end, the result is the same: a natural union of husband and wife by which they come together to perpetuate the human race according to God's plan and order. *It is good to understand the above, particularly if one is involved with someone from another race, culture, religion or legal jurisdiction.*

Success in marriage requires a large investment of love, compromise, time, honesty, and sacrifice for the greater benefit of the union in particular and the society as a whole. In the final analysis, you will find, all things being equal, that men and women throughout the world behave very much alike. The "battle of the sexes" still rages on fiercely in some parts of the world. In other parts, only "skirmishes" are fought.

It is a battle no sex can, or should, win. It is an ongoing battle, sometimes silent, which is fought in the bedrooms, living rooms, work place and other locations where males and females congregate. So, the earlier people *understand and respect* their sexual differences as created by God, the better for humanity. Outside the bedroom, women have been fighting for sexual equality with men for many centuries. They are winning, even if only slowly. Only very conservative and backward countries or states still keep women "under lock and key" for reasons best known to them. But they seem to forget that the tide is changing fast in favor of women's liberation. Human beings love freedom, and they exercise it sooner or later in one form or another.

Those who are happily married can pick up some points from this book and put them to good use, making their marriages even happier. For those separated or divorced, reading this book should lead them to think seriously of mending their ways and reaching some reconciliation with loved but separated ones. They should also be able to find out where and how things went wrong with earlier marriages. Thus, they have a chance of turning their previous marital *blitz* into marital *bliss* for the sake of their children and the larger society. As human beings, married couples and those courting or dating make mistakes, but they are expected to learn from these mistakes and make their lives happier.

To emphasize the importance of this topic, many points have been repeated time and time again. I hope this won't bother the reader.

One aim of this book, therefore, is to enable people, young and old, find happiness in their relationships by practising well-tested virtues <u>ab initio</u>. An almost step-by-step guide has been provided for the benefit of those without any experience in dealing with the opposite sex and who intend to start a relationship. Even experienced couples will be forced to rethink their ways and act more positively after reading this book. Points discussed here should help rejuvenate their marriages.

Dealing with the opposite sex has long been an art, which many people have sought to master. Males in particular should master it as they usually take the initiative to start relationships, as has been designed by nature. Exceptionally these days, some ladies, particularly the very well-to-do, have taken it upon themselves to woo men they fancy so as not to be left in the cold for long or even forever.

However, sexual deviants, like homosexuals, will certainly not enjoy reading this book except they change their sexual preference in favor of heterosexual relationships. But with time, counseling, and God's intervention, such deviants are expected to return to more natural sexual practices. Then and only then will they enjoy reading it and enjoy marital bliss as well.

This book is also full of fun, time-honored expressions, some history, some classic literary works, practical jokes, religious observances, and customary practices, thus making reading easy and interesting. Readers should add to the fun with stories, instances and experiences from their localities. Topical issues such as sexual harassment, abortion and rape have been included. Each chapter has been summarized in just a few words or sentences to enable the reader remember the key points.

Understandably, many people may not agree with suggestions made and points raised in this book. This disagreement should not be an issue. There are always many ways to solve a problem or reach an intended destination. As the saying goes, there are many ways to Rome, the eternal city. Such critics or dissenters are entitled to their views. While this may be so, readers are advised to read the book to the end in order to have a more balanced opinion about points or issues raised. They should take into account various cultural and religious practices and laws that are in place throughout the world and even within the same countries or localities.

Let me emphasize that this book is *only a guide* and is not intended to give text book solutions to specific problems in courtships or marriages. After all, since each courtship or marriage is unique, solutions to any problems within that relationship are expected to be unique in many ways. Thus, what works for a particular relationship may not work for another.

One last point I would like to make clear is that I have mixed American English and British English here and there as far as spellings go. There is really no confusion. It is just a matter of preference, having lived and schooled under both influences. For this, I ask the pardon of readers.

Because of sensitive matters discussed and the mature language and expressions used in this book, it is intended for those eighteen years and older.

Those who are currently happily married are expected to benefit from reading it and make their unions even happier. Those who have troubled relationships will see to what extent they can make things work for them again. Those who are newcomers to, or are contemplating, relationships are also advised to read it in order to be informed and be forearmed.

I therefore dedicate this book to all men and women who truly believe in marriage as a lifelong union and commitment and are doing their best to preserve this indissoluble, age-old institution. It is not easy. So also are other aspects of life.

With determination and commitment, reasonable success is assured.

Enjoy the book!

Albert C. Onochie, author

ACKNOWLEDGMENT

My sincere thanks go to my wife, Stella, for encouraging me to write a book on a topic I am familiar with. She provided a lot of information. Furthermore, she understood that at certain times I needed to be alone to concentrate well and do a good job. All I can say is, "I love you, darling. You have been a cornerstone in my life."

My children, Ikechukwu, Ifeanyi, Chiedu, Awele, and Uche were also very helpful in typing non-sensitive areas. I say to them all, "Thank you. May God continue to guard and guide you in all your endeavors."

Lastly, my gratitude goes to various people who helped my family in various ways when we came to the USA. They include Dr. Casimir I. Anyanwu, Dr. Berna Nwafor, Mr. Mike C. Oparaji, Mr. Emmanuel U. Amaefule, Mrs. Keny Amaefule, Nicholas A. Nuamah, Mr. Bobby Amah Amaefule, Ms Marian Osuji and Ms Beatrice Oparaji, etc. Their contributions are highly appreciated and remembered always.

May God bless them all!

Albert C. Onochie

Chapter 1

Natural Attraction between Male and Female

"Let us understand and appreciate our similarities and differences"

Beauty of the human body

Human beings are, many will agree, the most beautiful, the most intelligent, and the most complex of Almighty God's creatures in the entire universe currently known to man. God has given them control over all lower animals, other living things, and resources on land, air, and sea. However, in this process of controlling lower animals and other living things and resources, human beings have used these to a very selfish level, reaching the point where many animals and plants have since become extinct or are on the verge of becoming extinct. It was only in the last few centuries or so that man has begun to think seriously of his endangered environment. He has now seen the need and urgency to share it meaningfully and peacefully with other living creatures and things such as oceans, rivers, outer/inner space, and mountains, etc, in order to maintain the balance envisioned by nature.

A "normal human being" is a marvel to behold. His freewill apart, the entire body is so complex that no one clearly understands it. The human body is a wonder machine whose individual parts have been designed to perform specific functions and at the same time communicate with one another to ensure proper coordination of functions. Through the brain, all these functions are in perfect coordination, as seen in the workings of the respiratory system, digestive system, reproductive system, circulatory system, nervous system, the coordinated system of movements, the senses and more, and the symmetry and coordination between all these systems and senses. His freewill, which nobody apparently understands, directs him to do whatever he wants: to stand, sit, move in any direction, talk or

1

point his fingers, etc. He can also express his moods, based on changing situations and circumstances. One cannot but wonder how all these came to be.

Despite years of medical and other research works, not much is known about the total functioning of the human body. Only reasonable guesses can be made. Thus, artificial parts that have been used to replace damaged or lost parts of a human being have never been known to function as effectively as the original or natural parts.

The same view is held of lower animals and even plants. Nature is simply wonderful and mysterious. No one can completely unravel the secrets of creation or evolution as some scientists have postulated. Theories such as "The Big Bang" and "Evolution" from lower single-celled animals and apelike creatures millions (or thousands) of years ago abound. Theorists can continue to guess or speculate, but God in His infinite wisdom does not intend to reveal these secrets to mere humans, *to avoid evil and selfish manipulation of nature* as has been done since the time man appeared on the face of the earth.

Complementary roles of male and female

Christians and many others believe that God, as has been revealed in the Bible, made man (Adam) in His own image and likeness and "grafted" a woman (Eve) from Adam's rib, thus making her closely linked to him. God, in His infinite wisdom, saw it was good that man should not be alone. He therefore gave him a female companion, as written in the Bible—Genesis 2:17.

A man is not usually "complete" without a woman in his life, and a woman is usually not "complete" without a man in her life. The two are therefore complementary, according to God's will. Perhaps, the only notable exception may be those clerics who have made personal sacrifices and taken vows of chastity to remain celibate in order to serve God and humanity more effectively. There is therefore virtue in being celibate. The practice is probably as old as humanity. The Master, Jesus Christ Himself, showed a good example by being celibate and many people have followed. He even promised heavenly rewards for those who would forsake everything including marriage in order to follow him.

Paradoxically, a man and a woman appear to be like enemies who are inseparable and like friends who cannot work together. It is the spirit of compromise (give and take) that can keep them together for long, as *each person's interests and personality are usually diametrically opposite.* The abundant possession of the hormone *testosterone* by men generally seems to make them more active or cause them to behave in a way that pushes them to seek leadership or dominant roles, accept risky jobs, take sexual initiatives, and fight off potential rivals and pursue other ambitions. The noticeable suppression or little presence of this same hormone in women generally seems to make them passive most of the time. Again, nature designed this as a compromise to enable men and women come together and balance the forces of nature. Testosterone makes men have a high desire for sex and maintain a good erection, among other benefits. Its suppression in women makes them sexually passive and less interested in having sex. Imagine a world of men only or women only! What a dull world that would be!

2

Right from the time of creation, God intended that a man and a woman should stay together. Despite misunderstandings, quarrels, and rancorous situations, a man and a woman need each other and cannot escape this reality. A man may leave a woman today, but he soon finds himself in the embracing arms of another woman. In the same way, a woman may leave a man today, but she soon finds herself in the welcoming arms of another man. There must always be that natural attraction between a man and a woman, in the same way that unlike poles attract each other and in the same way that positive and negative charges must be brought together to produce light or electricity. Nature has so designed it that a man is *not usually* sexually attracted to another man and a woman is not usually sexually attracted to another woman. Were it not so, it would be impossible for humans to reproduce. In no time, the entire human race might cease to exist. Like virtually all rules, there are usually a few exceptions among sexual deviants who prefer homosexual or gay relationships.

A man and a woman are like a pair of scissors: separated, they are useless, but together they can work wonders. Both a man and a woman have *separate but com - plementary roles* in life. In this connection, God has given each of them power and resources to perform specific roles in life. Thus, apart from a few physical or anatomical differences in the areas of sex organs, breasts, body development, and appropriate hormones for specific functions, there is no physical difference between a man and a woman. Even though research has shown that the structure and anatomy of the male and female brain are different, this does not make one group superior to the other. Men are known to excel in logic and complex computations, while women are known to be more organized and confronting relationship problems, which men try to avoid. Expectedly, there are some exceptions. This observation is also true in the lower animal and plant kingdoms. While a man has some attributes that make him apparently superior to a woman, the latter equally has some attributes that make her apparently superior to a man. After all, it would be found that **no** sex is superior to the other. Both sexes are equally important. They have different but complementary roles to play in life. They cannot cheat or deceive nature for a long time, if at all.

However, women appear to have taken or been given a greater share of the burden of procreation and should therefore be given due respect for this. Consider the following phases: A woman "carries" her husband for at least ten to fifteen minutes during each of the average three to five sexual encounters needed for her to get pregnant; then she carries the pregnancy for eight to nine months, with all the sickness and inconvenience associated with pregnancy. In many parts of the world, a typical pregnant woman still works in the farm, cooks, washes up and engages in other domestic chores, etc, using old-fashioned methods. Despite all this, her husband may still ask her for sexual favors, and she will usually oblige him. If she does not, there may be no peace in the house for many days. Thereafter, she goes into life-threatening labor that lasts about four to six hours. She then suckles the baby for six to twelve months (as recommended by medical experts, who now see breast milk as better than Formula from the feeding bottle). This is done at a great cost to her body and shape. At night, she rarely sleeps, waking up when the baby cries or moves in order to pacify and/or feed him. She generally takes care of the child until the age of eighteen to twenty-one years.

What of her monthly periods and post-menopausal hot flashes? Multiply all of the above phases by the number of children a woman usually bears and you then begin to see how wonderful, tolerant, kind, supportive, and strong women really are. Can anyone then blame them when they make faces and have mood swings amidst all these problems?

Despite all this, some men humiliate and punish women, perhaps out of ignorance or sheer wickedness, or because of the abundant possession of testosterone.

Occasionally, however, some women are to be blamed for this abuse, as they cheapen themselves before men and their fellow women by engaging in husband snatching, gossips, naked modeling, and prostitution, among other recognized social vices. They expose their inner bodies (with little or nothing left to the imagination) for money in movies and other situations. They are also usually willing to do the unthinkable for monetary or other material benefits. Nature, perhaps, has reasons for making women this way and for making them carry this great burden of procreation. The biblical story of Adam and Eve and the circumstances under which God burdened Eve and her female descendants with childbirth are well known.

But what of lower animals, which go through this same process of sexual encounter, conception, birth and baby care, and even hunting for food for males as the big cats do? Was there any curse from God? The answer may never be known.

Different sexual behaviors worldwide

Sexual behavior is a complicated matter, at best, throughout the world. One may not understand or appreciate certain sexual behaviors in an environment unless one has been raised in that environment. Many behaviors that are acceptable to one society may be abhorred by another. This is hardly surprising, as the world itself is a complicated place to live in. Consider, for instance, the following complex matters:

Political systems and varieties throughout the world; religious bodies, groups and splinter groups, and varieties throughout the world; cultural and social settings throughout the world; legal systems throughout the world; varieties of democratic systems throughout the world, climatic differences throughout the world, etc.

All these have influenced sexual behaviors in various ways from time to time in various eras.

Thus, virtually all religious groups, political groups, peoples and cultures throughout the world have conflicting views, laws and practices with respect to general sexual behavior, marriage, divorce, premarital sex, homosexuality, adultery, use of contraceptives, teen sex and pregnancy and abortion, **etc**. It is extremely difficult, if not impossible, to get these various groups *to agree to even disagree* on these issues, with each group trying to impose its will on the weaker groups. People have had to learn to navigate all these systems and keep the love game alive, sometimes at a great risk to their lives. No system or group seems to have all the

4

answers, and cannot please both sexes in a most satisfactory way. Even within the same group, conflict exists, as various people try to interpret the laws or customary practices to suit their circumstances or inclinations. In so doing, they are just exhibiting their selfish human nature. Needless to say that this has led to the founding of various religious and social groups and factions and even splinter groups within factions. People are then easily deceived and ripped off. Unfortunately, there is no end in sight, all in the name of freedom of speech and expression and peaceful assembly.

Early understanding of the complementarity of a man and a woman is desirable in order to create a better atmosphere for each to perform their roles properly in God's scheme of things. It is also necessary at the early stages to understand that, despite the attraction between a man and a woman, there are forbidden or sexually undesirable relationships as given in the bible, other holy/religious books and as practised under various cultures and customary laws. This has become necessary in the interest of peace, good health and harmony in society. This well tested arrangement has helped the production of healthy children through avoiding *inbreeding*. Even many of the lower animals practise this, with the notable exception of *male goats*, which mate with their mothers, sisters, cousins, aunts, nieces and even the kids they have fathered, etc.

On the other hand, it is a different matter with elephants, lions, the primates, and some other mammals. You will see virtually all of them avoiding inbreeding by driving young males away from their groups and encouraging them to go to other distant groups or herds for mating purposes. This practice is also supported and favored by medical research. Medical reasons apart, inbreeding can lead to unnecessary jealousy among males in a home, with the strongest killing the weakest so as to have all the females to themselves. As is usually the case, there are exceptions among sexual or sick deviants who practise inbreeding in various forms. In this connection, some men have even come to the open to confess that they usually dis-virgin their daughters, while some women within the same households have also openly confessed to dis-virgining their sons, as a way of "introducing" them to sex matters. How sickening! How can *incest* be deliberately committed, with all the men and the women available for sex in the entire playing field? It is really sickening.

Generally, however, no society tolerates inbreeding or its notorious cousin, incest. The punishment and humiliation meted out to those caught are usually unbearable. In some parts of the world, men involved in this abominable practice have been known to commit suicide, as they could no longer bear the shame associated with their behavior.

In fact, the Bible's Old Testament Leviticus 18:6-18 expressly forbids various forms of incest: sex with a close relation, sex with parents, sex with a sister, sex with grand children, sex with an aunt, sex with a daughter in-law, sex with a brother's wife, and so on. Deuteronomy 22: 30 and St. Paul's letter in 1 Corinthians 5:1 also forbid sex with a father's wife.

As regards homosexuality, Leviticus 18:22 expressly forbids this behavior as follows: "You shall not lie with a male as with a woman; it is an abomination."

5

As regards sex with animals, Leviticus 18: 23 clearly states: "And you shall not lie with any beast and defile yourself with it, neither shall any woman give herself to a beast to lie with it; it is perversion."

You are free to check out all these in the Bible.

Forbidden or frowned-upon sexual liaisons

These **forbidden areas** include, but are not limited to:

sexual liaison with a son or a daughter, or with a father or a mother
sexual liaison with a very close cousin or any cousin at all
sexual liaison with an uncle or an aunt
sexual liaison with a brother or a sister
sexual liaison with step children or other step relatives
sexual liaison with a brother's wife or a sister's husband
sexual liaison with an uncle's wife or an aunt's husband
sexual liaison with a cousin's wife or husband
sexual liaison with a son's wife or daughter's husband
sexual liaison with a father's wife (in a polygamous setup)
sexual liaison with a married person
sexual liaison with a friend's wife or husband
sexual liaison with other close or blood relations
sexual liaison with underage persons or innocent children *entrusted* to one's care
sexual liaison with sick persons (e.g., the mentally imbalanced or patients in a medical or hospital environment)
sexual liaison with "masters" or "servants"
sexual liaison with in-laws
sexual liaison with a nephew's wife or a niece's husband
sexual liaison with a nephew or a niece
sexual liaison with dead persons
sexual liaison with animals
sexual liaison with "other persons" for various reasons.

Many more forbidden or undesirable sexual relationships can be added. It is therefore not an exhaustive list. The latter may look formidable or intimidating, but it is not so. Look around you and beyond and you will see it is a wide field that is left for you to "fish" in or explore. A very tiny fraction of it may not even be "explored" in one's lifetime. So, do not be tempted to go near any of these forbidden areas. Temptation is always present, particularly if there is no actual blood relationship, but it should be fought off. Such dangerous liaisons have been known to destroy lives and family units. However, in some countries, notably in the Middle East and Asia, cousins usually marry cousins and they have no qualms at all about this. This is done in the hope of keeping sons and daughters within the same family folds, so that they do not stray too far away. It also keeps costs of marriage down. This practice is an exception and not the rule, as far as forbidden sexual liaisons are concerned.

Also to be condemned or avoided is so-called modern day *wife-husband swap - ping*. Deviants, to be justified, now call this *extramarital adventure*. What a name! This is a very dangerous game, and it is bound to destroy families sooner or later. Similar to wife-husband swapping is *swinging*. Those who participate in this abominable activity are called swingers. This generally involves couples participating in open sexual activities with as many partners as possible at the same time and place, to the pleasure of watching and/or participating members. Needless to say that these sexual activities could bring jealousy among couples, pregnancy, and sexually transmitted diseases, among other dangers.

These sex deviants have invented a number of euphemisms in this game of sex:

Nocturnal emission (wet dream)

Sexual expression (masturbation)

Making love (having sex)

Blue movie (sexually explosive movie for adults only), etc.

There are many other euphemisms that cannot be mentioned here for the sake of decency. It is only when one moves in the circles of sex deviants that one may be in a position to understand their coded language; otherwise, one languishes in ignorance.

Despite all the men and women available for friendship, it is inconceivable that people can contrive to swap partners, throwing caution to the wind. The practice should be condemned and outlawed in its various forms, as it destroys the very basis of marriage and sex between a specific woman and a specific man in a union.

There is another form of wife-husband swapping. Under this arrangement or extramarital adventure, a number of married couples swap partners and even children in some extreme cases, either on an ad hoc or permanent basis, simply for sexual pleasure or variety. This arrangement, to say the least, debases the marriage institution as well as the fruits of that institution. This practice is also fraught with dangers, among which are the tendency for marriages to collapse and the possibility of incestuous relationships among children of swapping couples in future. These children may not be aware that they are the byproducts of parental swapping.

Of all the above forbidden sexual relationships, incestuous ones (involving very close blood relations, particularly parents and children or brothers and sisters) are the most damaging and the least tolerated by any society. In many societies, males involved may even be banished, if not killed outright. In others, "sacrifices" are offered to the "gods" to ward off evil while appropriate punishments are meted out to offenders.

Marriage or union with nonblood relations tends to produce stronger and more varied offspring, who are less susceptible to diseases and who genetically confuse enemies (including bacteria) that kill them.

Another area that needs to be mentioned (or rather criticized) is sexual relationships with people of the same sex (homosexuality) or even with animals. These are contrary to good conscience and offend human decency and God's laws. Thus, gay (for men) and lesbian (for ladies) relationships are to be condemned in whatever forms they are practised. They are even expressly forbidden by the Bible (Old Testament) and other holy books and by all decent societies the world over. **Thus, man to man, and woman to woman, sexual relationships are forbidden** and should never be practised under any circumstances. It is a very abnormal and condemnable practice. Sodomy or homosexuality is evil. It brought down great societies and empires of old. It is prevalent in today's societies, across the world, and stands ready to destroy the world morally. Freedom of expression and other human rights, which are practised in today's societies, have contributed immensely to this increasing moral laxity. People of the same sex are similar to "like poles," which ordinarily should repel each other, but here they attract each other, clearly against the laws of nature. Perhaps nature has a hand in all this, as elements of homosexuality have been observed in some lower animals and even some primates.

Similar to homosexuality is bi-sexuality. This means having sex with both sexes, all in the name of sexual freedom. This, to say the least, is contrary to natural laws and should be equally condemned.

At the other extreme is copulation with lower animals such as horses, goats, cows, dogs, etc. What can man not do? Imagine what freaks can result from this liaison: horseman, or manhorse, dogman or mandog, or something resembling a Minotaur in Greek mythology. Will the end result be treated as a man or an animal? Informal sources usually float rumors of having seen some soldiers and animal attendants have sex with animals. Nearer home, it is not unusual to hear of pet owners sleeping and actually having sex with their "beloved pets." This may not be surprising in some societies where some pets are sometimes regarded as being more important than, or at least equal to, human beings. All the same, many people believe that a line should be drawn between human beings and animals.

Another shocker is copulation with dead persons. Some people have reported witnessing this abomination, and one television program has actually featured a story of a man who kept a dead wife for some time and kept having sex with the corpse, even though rigor mortis had set in. It was later determined that the man was mentally imbalanced. In another development somewhere in Africa, a young man lost his wife soon after their marriage, on which he spent almost his entire life savings. Unfortunately, the marriage had not been consummated before she died. While mourners were wailing at the top of their voices, the husband asked them to excuse him to mourn his departed wife specially. So, he was left in the room alone with the wife's corpse. He closed the door behind him. But when he did not come out after a while, some mourners became worried that he might harm or even kill himself if he was not restrained. Some of them then opened the door and, to their astonishment, found the husband having sex with the dead wife. The embarrassment that followed is better imagined than experienced. Thereafter, the demented man shamefully left the vicinity and settled elsewhere.

It is recognized that, perhaps due to sex hormonal imbalance or malfunctioning of some genes, some human beings may be inclined to succumb to same-sex relationships. This is a problem that can be treated easily through counseling if only such deviants can come forward. Homosexuality is never tolerated in any decent society despite all invisible and sometimes visible benefits some adherents claim it brings to them. Supporting efforts or clamoring to legalize this practice, as some countries or states have done or are trying to do, is like trying to obtain from the back door what cannot be obtained through the front door, using the law as a stepping stone or support. One step usually leads to another. By taking one step after another, the whole process soon becomes uncontrollable and addictive, like being on drug.

Initially, homosexuals started by engaging in deviant sexual acts from behind closed doors where they covered their acts, too ashamed to be seen and too secretive to be suspected by "regular people." Then, they graduated into the next stage of advertising themselves in public and in the press in various ways. Finally, they decided to go "nuclear." They now go to court and even some churches to seek a marriage union of man and man or woman and woman. They even talk of adopting or having children through arrangements with "regular people." If this is their intention, why don't they then marry their opposite numbers? Hypocrisy or self-deceit is the answer.

The more informed or educated sexual deviants are the more ingenious their attempts to seek recognition in all aspects of life, including fighting discrimination against them, all in the name of freedom.

It may not be surprising in the not-too-distant future if sexual deviants decide to marry animals such as dogs, primates or other animals they may fancy, again all in the name of freedom. Freedom is being redefined daily by various people to suit their inclinations or personal lifestyles, no matter how weird or strange these appear to others. There is, therefore, the need for the law to move faster than the deviants in order to arrest these ugly situations now spreading like wild fire, particularly in so-called developed countries. Society is being gradually degraded or destroyed. Everybody should remember what happened to Sodom and Gomorrah in the Old Testament of the Bible.

In order to make a good partner, it is necessary to understand the nature of both sexes and the complementarity of both in God's scheme of things. Without this firm understanding one may not fully know why males or females behave the way they do. This understanding can be obtained from those who know better—parents, teachers, sociologists, doctors, social workers, priests etc. or from books and sheer observation of people around. So, start being a good lover or partner by understanding the differences and similarities between, and the complementarity of, both sexes.

Sex appeal and some characteristics of the sexes

It is also necessary for you to understand the sexual behavior of men and women in general. Both, expectedly, should possess *sex appeal,* which can only be defined by men or women themselves, as perceived by beholders. However, it can roughly be described as a form of natural attraction that is present in one sex and appeals to the opposite sex. What is sexually appealing to one man or woman may not be sexually appealing to another man or woman, even from the same cultural background or environment. This makes a clear-cut definition very difficult, as "one man's meat is another man's poison." A woman may be sexually appealing to a man by the way her body has been formed (her so-called "assets" in sexual circles). The same man could also be attracted by the way she generally looks or by the way she dresses, walks, makes up, talks, or even sends messages with her eyes and other parts of her body. These same actions or assets, however, may be repulsive to another man. In the same way, a man may be sexually appealing to a woman by the way he dresses, greets, laughs, plays games, does his job, or by his mere physique in these days of body building, with a lot of steroids and time on exercise machines. These same qualities may be repulsive to another woman. Thus, all animals of the same species are beautiful by their standards. Monkeys and human beings should not be compared. Each group is different. A gorilla will definitely prefer a gorilla baby to a human child.

Generally, men are more sexually active, outgoing, and like to boast to friends about their "sexual conquests." This may sound childish, but men have reasons for behaving this way. Women play hard to get and any man that succeeds in wooing and taking them to bed is seen to have done a seemingly difficult task such as untying the Gordian Knot or crossing the Rubicon.

Women, on the other hand, are generally sexually passive and like to be seen as preserving their modesty, chastity or purity, so as not to be called socially unacceptable names such as "loose" or "cheap," which tend to degrade or lower their standing before people. Nature itself, by placing the *hymen* in the vagina, probably intended that this should be used as a check on a woman's modesty, chastity, or fidelity. The hymen or "seal" is not usually broken except a woman has had sex. It is not known if the hymen can be accidentally broken, as some have claimed. Perhaps scientists need to research this and lend support to women who appear to be in this category. This is also another burden on women, which is absent in men.

As far as sex is concerned, however, it is usually not possible to tell how many times a man or a woman has had it, or the extent to which a sex organ has been used. If the information were readily available, it would be possible to be more discriminating in the choice of a partner, particularly when choosing a female partner. All the same, it is only in the case of a girl that one can say that she has been "disvirgined" if the hymen is broken. There is no such burden on a man. Perhaps, some day, plastic surgeons may be able to help out by reinstating the hymen and restoring virginity to promiscuous ladies who are looking for husbands. But one may be haunted by one's conscience and may not keep the secret for long.

So, it is possible for a lady to claim that she has had sex only two or three times even if she has had it ten times over, as there is no measuring instrument. A man is even luckier, as he can claim not to have had sex at all. There is no way to check this out, particularly if any evidence has been washed off.

Of course, virginity no longer seems to be a virtue and a "must" before a marriage is consummated in some societies. In other societies, it is still held in high esteem and even celebrated. However, there are indications that modern girls are fast returning to the "virgin era" for various reasons, including easier marketability among eligible bachelors, fear of pregnancy from irresponsible men, and fear of contracting sexually transmitted diseases from casual sex partners, particularly in these days of debilitating diseases such as AIDS. This is the way nature has made females, in sharp contrast to males.

Also notice that females generally have softer and more rounded bodies and bigger buttocks, have softer voices, have little or no hair on their bodies, and conduct themselves more gently. Contrast these with men's rugged builds, almost flat buttocks, deep voices, rigid muscles, hairy bodies, large frames, and rough behavior. With all these different attributes, men and women easily attract one another, just like "unlike poles," which attract one another.

Due to increasing levels of promiscuity and moral laxity in today's societies, however, every man, after messing around with so many women, wants to be *the first love* of the woman he finally chooses as his wife. His ambition is understandable, to ensure that his wife hasn't slept around before going to bed with her and "claiming" her forever. Appropriately too, every woman, after having messed up a lot in her bid to secure a husband, wants to be *the last love* of the man she finally chooses as her husband. Her position is understandable. This is to ensure that her philandering husband does not set his eyes again on other women. But this is utopian or mere wishful thinking for both the man and the woman. If you want a virgin for a partner, then remain a virgin yourself.

Women by nature are generally possessive. They like to be attached to, or be associated with, one man throughout their lives. Polyandry (having more than one husband at the same time) is virtually unknown in all societies and it is not likely to succeed because of the very nature of women themselves. Their genetic make-up does not allow for this. It is so too in the lower animal kingdoms. But men are polygamous and philanderous by nature and love to have freedom to "deal" with as many women as possible. Since men can no longer easily marry more than one wife in some countries, they have come around the "problem or obstacle" by marrying one woman legally and keeping girlfriends or mistresses at the same time. Thus, their illicit and multiple sexual liaisons have continued, but in a different way. Even in some societies and some religions that permit polygamy, some men marry more than one wife, say three or four wives, and still maintain girlfriends or mistresses around them.

Between these extremes are men who are passive and women who are sexually active, some of the former becoming almost sexually dead and some of the latter becoming flirts and prostitutes. Apparently, this is a good natural balancing act to ensure a not-too-active sexual situation that could lead to over-population and a not-too-passive sexual situation that could seriously deplete population. Thus, about 80 to 90 percent of men can be said to be sexually active while roughly the same percentage of women can be said to be sexually inactive or passive. In this way, these men must go to these women to convince them to have sexual relations with them. This is not usually an easy task, but that is one of nature's ways of controlling population growth. At the other extreme are men (10 to 20 percent) who are sexually passive but rely on being approached or coaxed by sexually active

11

women (10 to 20 percent) for sexual liaisons. This is another balancing act of nature.

There is always a balance in nature in all our actions. No one fully understands this. One action produces an equal but opposite reaction as in the law of motion taught in physics.

It is therefore necessary for both sexes to understand the nature of sexual behavior as modified by society and learn to make good companions during courtship and good couples when they marry.

Perhaps, before leaving this subject of sexuality among animals, it is good to mention the weird world of sexual behavior and characteristics within the lower animal kingdom.

Some species change sexes if one sex is in short supply, to ensure some balance. This is common among clown fish.

Male sea horses, rather than females, carry pregnancies to full term. Some families of slugs and earthworms are hermaphrodites, i.e., having both male and female sexual organs at the same time.

At the other extreme, cannibalism is exhibited by some species during or immediately after mating, e.g., the praying mantis and some spiders. The female usually eats up the male.

For other species, sexual encounter is like a battle, as males brutalize females, and sometimes this even ends in the death of the females. Examples can be seen in the mountain sheep, Hawaiian monk seals and some frogs.

Fortunately or unfortunately, the human species, the <u>Homo sapiens</u>, is perhaps a little bit of each of these behaviors or characteristics. Even with tough imprisonment terms and capital punishment, human beings are not deterred in their ill-treatment of the opposite sex or their better halves. The struggle for a better society, where love reigns and where each sex appreciates and respects the opposite sex, continues.

Highlights

Appreciate the human body. Do not abuse it unreasonably.

Understand the similarities and the differences between the sexes, including their peculiar behavior.

Appreciate and respect the opposite sex.

Enjoy sex life abundantly, but be sure to observe laid down taboos or "no-go" areas and any personal constraints.

Chapter 2
Meeting a Future Partner

"Make your choice and stick to it."

Possible meeting places

There is no magic formula for meeting a future partner. There is also no special place or spot where a possible future partner can be found waiting to be picked up. There is apparently no readymade future partner for anybody. It is a combination of luck and your efforts, at the very least. You may look without seeing, listen without hearing, or even walk past him or her without knowing or following up.

If Mother Luck shines on you, then you may meet your future partner with little or no effort. If not, you may have to search for long. It won't be easy. In the meantime, relations and friends may bring pressure upon you (if you are getting too old) before you decide to make your choice, no matter the imperfections.

How then can one meet one's future partner? And in exactly what circumstances can this happen?

Many people unknowingly meet their future partners almost daily. Yet they fail to react or take the first positive steps. Future partners are found everywhere:

    at conferences or conventions
    in churches and other places of worship
    in schools and offices
    in buses, trains, and airplanes
    in shopping malls, Laundromats and supermarkets
    at weddings and other social events
    in hospitals
    along streets and in neighborhoods

in libraries
in hotels and holiday resorts
in recreation centers, swimming pools and other public places
in friends' or relations' houses.

There is also the now popular computer dating service, as well as the **Internet** through which people of like qualities, interests, or backgrounds are brought together through exchange of some correspondence and perhaps pictures. Pictures from these sources are very deceptive, as one may be dealing with a cripple or a dwarf or someone whose age has been hidden by makeup and other manipulative practices. Thus, indirect meeting through the Internet or computer dating has serious disadvantages, as you do not have the opportunity to see your "proposal" in person before making up your mind. Some people might have succeeded in meeting the right partners through these media.

However, you should remember that you could be dating a blind person or someone else with disabilities, which you cannot put up with. Despite this quick connection and ease of phone communication, these media do not compare with meeting someone face to face and deciding almost instantly if there is any attraction, or if any relationship is likely to work out.

Nightclubs and "joints" and such similar places may not be good places to meet a future partner because of the usual laxity that pervades the atmosphere and poor lighting. No one would like "to buy a pig in a poke" except those looking for an opportunity to rip off their partners and run away.

Despite the almost innumerable places mentioned above, it may still be difficult for one to come across a possible future partner. The problem may relate to the fact that one may not know exactly what qualities to look out for in a future partner. One thing, however, is certain. Except one tries, one can never succeed. Thus, the first step is to find out if one needs a future partner. Do you need a partner or not? If the answer is no, then there is no problem to solve, as the problem will have solved itself. Perhaps you still have a lot of time ahead of you, unlike if you are in your late thirties or so.

However, if the answer is yes, then there are so many points and issues to consider. These may take considerable time and effort to sort out, but in the end the exercise will be quite rewarding. Young men and women usually have good, and perhaps utopian, ideas about their future partners. However, as they grow older and move toward marriage, they find that they must adjust their utopian requirements in the light of what is actually available or possible out there.

General qualities expected of a partner or mate

What kind of a partner does one need? What should your soul mate have to make you happy?

The answer is not easy, as one soon discovers. Defining what you want in a future partner helps considerably to *narrow down your search*. This is similar to what the police do in criminal profiling and in their search for suspects. This approach saves a lot of time and resources. You cannot search for a soul mate forever.

Here, however, are a few points, among others, for consideration:

Tall, average, medium height, or a short partner (if someone actually wants this size).

Fair-complexioned, black, white, or colored otherwise.

College-educated, high school educated or semi-illiterate.

Slim-build, fat, or *average size all over*, from head to foot.

Beautiful, handsome, or average look.

Poor or humble background, royalty or average background.

Brown-haired, blond or brunet or black-haired (with long or short hair).

Straight-legged, bow-legged, or long-legged.

Nurse, teacher, doctor, hair stylist, entertainer, actor/actress, sex model or office executive, masseur/masseuse, politician, professional gambler, musician, athlete, etc.

General sex appeal: dress style, manner of walking, talking, eating, singing, general poise, etc.

From Africa, Asia, Latin America, North America, Europe, or Australia.

A virgin or a "fairly experienced girl" (for a man)

Interracial and inter-tribal relationships are to be encouraged, as so much discrimination in the world could be reduced through this process. These relationships could also promote understanding and harmony among various races and tribes. However, you should ensure that colloquial phrases, jargons, or expressions that are peculiar to a group are not used at the beginning of a relationship, to ensure clear understanding between partners. You should use words or expressions that are well known, and then gradually explain any peculiar expressions or slangs to your partner.

Incidentally, in this game of sex, nobody usually wants someone who is experienced or who has failed a lot with members of the opposite sex. Everyone, particularly a man, wants someone who is fresh or new in the game. This is an "industry" where experience is an obvious disadvantage, unlike regular employment where experience is usually called for and appreciated.

As can be seen, the list of requirements is almost endless and can be a tall order to fulfil. Perhaps these sound utopian. They may not necessarily be so. <u>But it is important for people to have in their minds exactly what they want and work towards finding their heart's desire or someone very close to it.</u> Some people have been known to join clubs, societies, churches, and organizations in order to have the opportunity of talking to those they admire. There is nothing wrong with this approach. Where someone cannot find exactly what they want (and it is almost impossible to find exactly what one wants), they must come up with necessary compromises by making adjustments here and there in order to balance some requirements against others.

Remember that no one is readymade from heaven or born perfect, and no one is likely to have all good or desirable qualities. Even then, many qualities may not be known or decided upon until one becomes familiar with, or comes close enough to, a chosen partner. In this connection, the state of one's health, family history, temperament, and behavior may not even be gleaned from the first few meetings. This must be so, as a new acquaintance cannot easily be asked if there is a health or family problem. Sometimes a simple observation of an acquaintance (without any questions being asked) will tell a lot of stories about him or her. If you like someone who is slim and you find one, there is no assurance that he/she will remain slim forever. In the case of a woman, there is no assurance that her chest will not obey the natural law of gravity after some years of fondling by her husband and suckling by her babies. After all, what goes up must come down, through aging and other natural and unnatural causes.

Incidentally, the same thing applies to a man, who may find it difficult to maintain his usual erection after some years. The law of gravity works here, too; hence, it is necessary to pay more attention to *character* and *inner qualities* rather than outward appearances such as beauty and shape. A lady could combine beauty, brains and good character and be lucky to meet the right man. At the other extreme, a beautiful and shapely lady could be of bad character and end up not getting married because no man wants to put up with her behavior, while a lady who is not quite attractive but is of good character, by one's definition, could end up marrying the right man. So, beauty, though good to behold and appreciate, should not be given any undue priority. Like money, which is said to be the root of all evils, beauty is simply transient, but character and other invisible assets do last long and make marriages enjoyable. Ladies looking for long-lasting relationships should discountenance money possessed by men and should instead look out for inner, lasting qualities. As the saying goes, you should not judge a book by its cover; wait until you have read it. In like manner, wait until you have been with someone for some time before you make up your mind and judge him or her.

But first things should come first. Thus, every opportunity should be seized to get close to someone desired. Where people have been formally introduced, this becomes easier as the introduction can be followed up through phone calls or dates. In fact, some information about a person can be discreetly obtained from whosoever made the initial introduction. This information helps in reaching further decisions. Naturally, men should follow up and not expect women to do so, as the latter are not supposed to be so forthright or bold in making approaches, lest they be called "cheap" or be thrown away like dirt. This approach also gives some dignity to the lady (the man's desire).

Where no formal introduction is possible and a man sees a lady he seems to like, he should try to get close and start off a conversation of interest to her, perhaps on general matters first, in line with Dale Carnegie's book <u>How to Win Friends and Influence People.</u> Essentially, what this book suggests is that if you want someone to be interested in you instantly, you should discuss matters of utmost interest to the person such as his/her achievements, personal attributes, aspirations, and other good aspects of the person's life. Do not monopolize any discussion. Talk about the person and their interests and not about yourself. Do not monopolize a conversation. Be a good listener.

Initial problems and rebuffs

There may be an initial rebuff from the lady. This is perfectly normal, as ladies cannot be expected to say "yes" to all men who come asking for their hands in friendship. Even second and third attempts by a man at starting a conversation with his dream girl may meet with dismal failure, with his heart panting. Again, this is normal. He should not feel disappointed for long and should be prepared to keep trying. If he is lucky, the cold rebuffs or failures may begin to thaw out. This should be followed up gradually but steadily, lest one's initial intention be misread or mis-interpreted by the lady.

For many male beginners, there may be initial "stage fright" and lack of confidence. This is normal and is a part of growing up. It even happens in the lower animal kingdoms. Males who try to mate with females persist and eventually win them over. Persistence pays. As shall be seen later, there are reasons for this initial rebuff from females. Over time, males acquire more confidence. Talking to females then becomes easy and a lot of fun.

By the way, the earlier rebuffs are not unconnected with a woman's interest in buying time to find out a lot about the man before hand, and then be well armed or prepared before the next encounter with him. She therefore tries to find out if the man is serious with his proposal (or just trying to have only a good time). She also tries to find out if the man can withstand disappointments, lapses or failures in life, as well as if the man is tolerant and has a large heart to accommodate her occasional tantrums in real life situations and if he is from a good background, among other matters that are of interest to her.

Various approaches for male and female

Those in colleges or mixed high schools have the best chance of understanding themselves and overcoming shyness usually associated with male beginners. Once a male and a female become acquainted, picking up conversation or going out on a date becomes very easy. Where his dream lady belongs to a club or society that is open to all, the man should join so as to get closer to her. If she is living in an area that is well known and open, perhaps passing through there regularly may create an opportunity for the man and woman to come together. Again, if she is in a public vehicle such as a bus or a train, coming down with her at the same time and place may bring the man and the woman closer some day. There are so many scenarios for a man to explore, but what is important is to find out how to meet or get acquainted with his dream girl.

For girls, meeting their dream boys or men is much more tasking, as the first approach usually should come from males. Moreover, girls are not all that adventurous and may not have opportunities or freedom usually available to boys. This inhibition, fortunately or unfortunately, is gradually breaking down in developed countries. This is partly because of the serious effort (legally enforceable) not to discriminate between the sexes, who are regarded as equal in virtually all spheres

17

of life. As a result, some women now go out alone, unescorted—even to previously forbidden places—and pick up new relationships along the way. There used to be a saying: "What a man can do, a woman can equally do." Now, this saying has been recast as follows: "What a man can do, a woman can do, even better." All the same, not much has changed, as a majority of females still wait for males to make the first approach, open car doors for them, and lead the way in times of danger. This is only natural.

If a girl likes a boy, however, she should get as close as possible to him, so he notices her and then takes over the rest of the "relationship job." Boys, who welcome any opportunity to be close to girls, do not easily rebuff them, if at all. A girl can get closer to a boy by asking questions during or after classes. She can ask for directions from a boy and even request that she be escorted to dangerous or distant places. She can also reach a boy she likes through acquaintances and her own brothers or relations. In fact there are many ways that girls can follow to reach out to boys without cheapening themselves through flaunting and showing off their partially naked bodies (breasts, hips, and belly buttons, shoulders, etc.) or throwing their buttocks around seductively. These days, many girls are encouraged to wear skimpy dresses when they see what happens in Hollywood movies and at the annual award ceremonies. On these occasions, scantily dressed actresses leave almost nothing to the imagination, before a large audience, with the entire world also watching. They appear to compete with one another for the Most Naked Woman Award. It is good for ladies to realize that if they cheapen themselves by flaunting their "assets" in very immoral ways, they might end up being used as rags and thrown out by men.

Many decent approaches by girls have resulted in successful marriages, so girls should not remain in the cold on account of shyness, but should take one step at a time to ensure that their dream men have noticed them. There is no harm in trying for a male or a female. You cannot succeed unless you try and even try again and again.

In many societies in Asia, Latin America, and Africa, some families do early introductions, so that eligible bachelors and spinsters do not stray beyond certain boundaries to seek spouses. Generally, such early betrothals work out and have contributed considerably to stability within many societies or families. Unfortunately, this is a culture that is dying out gradually, as the world becomes smaller through increased urbanization, movements across cultural lines, and the increasing liberalization of human rights and choices across the globe, among other factors.

Thus if a boy or a girl is of marriageable age, he/she should start to consider matters relating to their possible future partners. The way to proceed will depend on the circumstances of each case or situation. Remember at all times that no person has all the qualities one may want in a partner, so be ready to make compromises and tradeoffs. Do not procrastinate, for time waits for no one. Moreover, someone else who is more serious may snatch your dream lady or man before you make up your mind, to your eternal regret.

You must go out and seek out the person you would like to get acquainted with. You do not expect any one to come knocking at your door saying "Here I am. I have all the qualities you are looking for." Thus, if you want a nurse or a doctor for a partner, go to hospitals or places where they congregate. If you want a teacher for a partner, go to schools to find one. If you want to have a "blue-blooded person," or a celebrity for a partner, move within the circles where they can be found. However, you need a lot of luck and prayers to reach your dream partner, who may have body guards with bulging muscles. Even if you find one, you need a lot more prayers and luck to survive in that relationship, as you may be regarded as the under dog and treated accordingly. This ill treatment may lead the disadvantaged or aggrieved partner to look for satisfaction elsewhere. In no time, such marriages or liaisons pack up because there was no real love between partners, just infatuation. No true foundation was laid for a lasting relationship. When such liaisons collapse, the underdogs seize the opportunity to reveal a lot about the relationships through selling their stories to newspapers, or writing books for payments running into several million dollars or the equivalent. Remember, too, that it is far easier for the proverbial camel to pass through the eye of the needle than for marriages of celebrities to succeed. Statistics and stories confirm this. Members of royal families, actors, actresses, athletes, and other celebrities have not been spared this marital blitz.

If you want a Brazilian or an Indian for a partner, go to where you can find them. You can, if time and money permit, undertake trips to the real places and have a wider range of choice than from home sources. But, please, do not look for an angel because you won't find one among human beings. Therefore, be more mundane in your search for, and choice of, a partner. With luck on your side, you are sure to find someone with whom you can share your future together.

However, if after a long search you cannot find anyone, you need to examine yourself very closely (and, perhaps, see a psychiatrist) to ensure that you are normal. Perhaps your requirements are out of the ordinary and may need to be modified in the light of what is really available or possible. If your requirements are out of the ordinary, you may never find a partner and you may end up a lonely person. Remember, too, that all human beings and animals have been genetically programmed to look out for certain traits in their future or sex partners. The rules of attraction seem to cut across all races and cultures. However, like all rules, there are *exceptions*. Sometimes one finds women loving men with abnormal traits, such as murderers and rapists, even murderers of their own children or spouses. This is also common in the lower animal kingdom, particularly among the big cats whose conquering males (after defeating the reigning male in a pride) kill off young babies of females in the pride. They then mate with those females almost immediately, to enable them to father their own offspring. In the same way, there are men who love women who have killed their children and who are generally not good mothers. This is nature at work, a mixture of weird and normal behavior, to keep everything in balance.

Considerations for a man

Now, what are those qualities one is likely to look out for in a future partner? In this kind of matter, it is really difficult to be "dogmatic", as what appeals to one person may not even move another. However, in general terms, the following points, among others, should be considered by a man, in addition to those mentioned earlier in this chapter:

A girl's outward features and appearance
Family background and traits
Educational background and home training
A girl's manners and mood swings
Possibility of good motherhood
Likelihood of 100% faithfulness to him
History of previous marriages in the girl's family etc.

Considerations for a woman

In like manner, a girl looking for a future partner, or who is being "toasted" should watch out for these qualities in a man, among others, in addition to those earlier mentioned in this chapter:
Educational background and leadership qualities
Exhibition of patience and "sculptured" body
Gentility in manner
Ability to provide for, and protect, the family.
Capability of shouldering family responsibilities
Possibility of good fatherhood and transfer of healthy genes to offspring
Status in general, etc.
Family background and traits

Status means a lot to women, and they look out for this in a man they intend to live with. Status means a lot of things—money, ambition, profession, position in society, power, modesty, talent, etc. In ancient times, a good and brave hunter, soldier, or wrestler could be compared today to a politician, an engineer, a doctor, an athlete, or a business executive. The "status" requirement changes from generation to generation and from one locality to another, but the meaning is still the same—one's standing or influence in society.

Sex appeal is too subjective a quality to be listed here, as what appeals to Mr. G or Miss A may not appeal to Mr. B or Miss P. As the saying goes, "One man's meat is another man's poison." Men and women, with adjustments or tradeoffs here and there, usually seek all the above qualities and more. This has been so from time immemorial. Even in the case of lower animals, females look for the "best males" to mate with, to ensure they have strong offspring that can survive the harsh realities of jungle life. How natural and sensible!

As mentioned earlier, no one is an angel, Adonis, Aphrodite, Venus, beautiful Helen of Troy, or Cleopatra. Even Hollywood's created beauty, or any other female artificially made very beautiful by organizations that specialize in this kind of activity will soon fade away, while only what nature has given remains. *So make your choice carefully and thereafter stick to it.* Be a man—<u>Esto Vir.</u> Be committed and be responsible. If you keep changing your mind, you may end up being "a rolling stone that gathers no moss." Perhaps, by the time you know it, you are out of the market for consideration as a partner, due to age and other factors. Are actors, actresses, athletes, and other celebrities listening?

Highlights

Your future partner is everywhere; just open your eyes and try your luck.

Find out those qualities that appeal to you most before searching for a partner. This helps to narrow down your search and save time.

Go to the right places, pick up one, and stick to your choice unless there are good and tenable reasons for effecting a change.

Be *mundane* in your ambition and requirements, as no one is an angel.

Chapter 3

Serious Courtship (or Dating) and Background Checks

"It is better to have loved and lost than not to have loved at all."

Courtship (or dating) and how to go about it

Courtship, or dating as some people choose to call it, means different things to different people. Some see it as an opportunity to know the other person very well and explore the possibilities of marriage. Some see it as an opportunity only to have a good time—the man seeking sexual satisfaction and the woman seeking it, as well as some material things of life from him. Still, others see it as an activity or responsibility that should eventually lead to the altar. If both parties make their **intentions** known early enough, they may decide to go ahead with the relationship or break it up if there is no meeting of the minds or what attorneys call **consensus ad idem**—an essential ingredient in the law of contract.

In this discourse, it is intended to treat only serious courtship that could lead to the altar or registry through developing and nurturing the relationship all the way.

Various practices worldwide

After spotting or identifying a possible future partner as indicated earlier, it is now the man's responsibility to start necessary courtship or serious dating. Largely gone are the days when ladies or wives, sometimes without having seen the pictures of their prospective husbands, had to be "posted" or "parceled" to their husbands in "foreign lands." Some people have dubbed this practice "marriage by post" or "mail-order bride arrangement." Nevertheless, it is still practised, in various forms, in many parts of the world including so-called developed nations where some people use the medium of the Internet and specialized organizations to reach out to those they wish to establish some relationship with. This looks like using modern or new tools to re-establish old practices. So, nothing seems to have changed.

Thus in "those days," it was the practice in many countries and cultures to marry first (without dating or courtship) and start loving one's partner rather perfunctorily later. *That is, courtship and intimacy took place after marriage rather than before.* Generally, there was no question of love. It was like people saying: "Whatever is arranged is good for me."

Thus, as soon as the "mail-order bride" was "delivered" to the anxiously waiting and possibly sex-starved husband, the latter commenced his "matrimonial duties" the same night. Cases of "rejects" were unheard of or quite insignificant. However, in one notable case, as the story is told, a husband rejected his bride-to-be because the "male courier" or escort had "tampered" with her. The escort had asked to be rewarded "in kind" for his services, and he accordingly had consensual or coerced sex with the bride. This action, today, could qualify, or go on trial, as rape.

Modern people may laugh at this arrangement, but it worked very well for people of that time. Couples involved in this kind of arrangement trusted the judgment of people on both sides who knew each other's family members very well. Such marriages were family or community-based and worked very well. Among the many benefits claimed, in-laws were close to one another and helped out in times of difficulties. They also ensured that husbands did not maltreat wives and that the latter were faithful, as they were closely watched.

Modern ways of courtship and marriage have their flaws. If our ancestors were to come back to life, they would certainly condemn what is on the ground now and praise their own times. That is life. Each generation thinks their time was better than the one after theirs.

However, with increasing awareness around the world, increasing urbanization, and extension of liberties and education and the breakdown of social and customary barriers and practices, people have since begun to pick their own spouses rather than accept anything "arranged" or "parceled." Whether this new approach has led to instability in homes and insecurity of marriages is highly debatable. The point remains, however, that in those societies where arrangements of this sort are still practised or where family members have a voice in the choice of partners for their loved ones, marriages have been known to be far more stable and long lasting.

There are various ways for a man to date or court a girl of his choice. In some Western nations or cultures, he could get in touch with his date by phone, through the Internet or letter, or through appointments in parks, coffee shops, swimming pools, restaurants, etc. without being seriously noticed or disturbed by anybody. This is a culture that has developed over the years and is known to work most of the time. In other societies or circumstances, however, personal visitation may be embarked upon, there being no other way to reach her. Other rendezvous such as riverside, marketplace, or office may be too open, while a farm or any other hidden rendezvous will elicit a lot of suspicion from the relatives of the girl, for fear of the latter being violated or harmed in any way.

It is extremely important for the man to be of age in his locality so that he can always bear the full consequences of his actions. There are usually so many age variations from locality to locality, even within the same tribal or linguistic grouping. The man should not run foul of the law – civil or customary.

In the "good old days," men got married in their mid-twenties or early thirties because of the need to be mature, self-supporting and educated in handling marital problems. These days, men get married much earlier, just as they are being "weaned" from the feeding bottle. This usually results in early, acrimonious divorce and an uncertain future. There should be no hurry about marriage as long as a man is below thirty and the woman is below twenty-five. A man should be able to support himself, have self-discipline, learn some patience and have reasonable education or training before getting married. He will then have equipped himself to deal with the various presentations or facets of married life.

A woman, too, should be self-supporting and know a lot about men's behavior and family life before becoming a wife. The age of fulltime housewives (waiting on their husbands' incomes) appears to have gone for good.

At this juncture in the relationship, the man should try to be a "one-woman" man and the woman a "one-man" woman, to avoid any suspicion from one's partner who may be jealous and take action to disrupt the relationship. Courtship should be taken seriously. Both partners should give various *tests* along the way to ensure the chosen partner is the right one for him or her. There should be no pretence about this. This is all about your life and future.

Disclosure of information

While courting or dating, one should be sincere, telling the truth about one's life, home, workplace, likes and dislikes, blood relations, friends, medical or health history, favorite foods, and clothes. Other disclosures should include future plans, ambitions, hobbies, fears, religious inclination, parenthood, educational background and schools attended, age, previous relationships (if thought necessary or asked), and any other information likely to be of interest to one's partner. In short, one should mention everything one's partner should know, to enable him or her decide whether "to be" or "not to be." All these disclosures should be made gradually, perhaps within the space of six to twelve months, which is the *minimum time* recommended for courtship, before marriage. These disclosures are very important since no one would like to marry from a family with crippling or hereditary diseases, or where spouses are battered and thrown out with ease or which has a history of socially shameful acts.

Because of the existence of crippling and hereditary diseases, it is necessary for an intending couple to undergo medical tests, know their blood groups and genotypes and other special medical conditions. Thereafter, their doctor should advise them as to their suitability as partners in marriage. If the medical tests show adverse results, the risk is theirs to take. Thus, it is not advisable for a man and a woman who are both "AS" (sickle cell disease *carriers*) to get married because of the high chance of producing children who are "SS" (full-fledged sicklers). There should be no sentiment about this, as any medical problems later discovered could cripple a marriage socially or spiritually, except perhaps they were disclosed at some point during courtship.

In some cultures, background checks will be made as to whether family members belong to secret societies or practise witchcraft or other evil sciences. Many other issues will also be examined, including burial practices, financial responsibilities, good manners and the practice of female circumcision in particular. *Information about a person can also be obtained from classmates, coworkers, neighbors, friends and organizations to which he/she belongs.* This is expected to be done discreetly, to avoid any embarrassment.

During this period of courtship, there will be exchange of visits at appointed and non-appointed times. Phone calls can be made; cards and flowers or even gift items can be sent, to emphasize the flow of love between those dating. Love letters, suitably worded, may be sent, but one must be sure not to commit oneself yet, until there is certainty for advancement to the next higher stage in the love affair. In some cultural settings, the man may render services to his future in-laws by way of working in their farms periodically or assisting in other ways. On the other hand, in some Western countries, cards sent on important dates and events are quite appropriate. In this way, the relationship between the parties (as well as the marriage at a later stage) waxes stronger.

As the relationship becomes stronger, it is advisable for both parties not to insist on appointments before visiting, in order to remove any suspicion of infidelity. When the woman visits, she should look around to see if she can render any assistance in cleaning up the house or apartment or even cooking for her loved one. Doing this shows she is homebred and can fit into the man's life. In this way, she gradually becomes a part of the man's life. Likewise, the man should be able to assist his loved one in running some errands that are tedious, or escorting her to places for protection purposes. In this way, he becomes a part of her life. Women appreciate this very much.

Intimacy (or anticipation of sex) during courtship

At this point in the relationship, sex should be ruled out to avoid any complications and possible embarrassment to the girl's family. However, "light kisses" where practised, holding hands, and touching non-sensitive areas could be permitted in order to further strengthen the relationship. Both parties should be conscious of going too far, as one thing or step could lead to the next and before one would say "Jack Robinson," they could find themselves in bed having sex. Depending on their level of self-discipline, the couple could touch "sensitive areas" in a responsible way to enable each one have a "feel" of what the other has and how responsive they are to very sensitive touches. In this way, a woman can attempt to find out if her man has the "right size" of penis, if this aspect of the relationship is very important to her. Generally, women love men who are "reasonably endowed." Size itself does not actually matter as long as the penis is active and he can satisfy her sexually when it is put to good use. Thus, a woman should not be unduly alarmed or afraid if her man is on the large side or is "generously endowed," as her vagina has been made by nature to accommodate any man's size after proper lubrication, excitement, or foreplay.

In the same way, a man can easily find out if his loved one has the "right size" of breasts and other natural endowments. Again, size does not matter. However, some men like large size, some like medium size, but a great majority do not like very small breasts because there is almost nothing to fondle.

Staying overnight in your spouse's home is not advisable, to avoid any temptation to have sex and possibly destroy the natural likeness for each other. *Let sex continue to be anticipated until the right moment.* There should be no cheating on one's spouse while abstinence is practised. Generally men and an increasing number of women these days "reserve" or do not touch their spouses when courting but engage in wild sex with others. This is an extremely dangerous game in view of the possibility of contracting STDs and even falling out of favor with loved ones, thus breaking up a beautiful relationship. Ladies who are virgins should try to remain so until the right moment, particularly if their lovers already know this. If a girl loses her virginity to the wrong man at the wrong time and place, she has in effect "sold" her soul to him. This could haunt her conscience for life. Virginity is a virtue that is valued by parents and prospective husbands. In fact, in ancient times, husbands of virgins had to reward their parents in-law. Other celebrations announcing the wives as virgins followed. For those celebrations, white pieces of cloth, which had been used to clean up during the first sexual encounter, were conspicuously displayed with bloodstains on them. Parents should therefore protect their daughters by encouraging them to remain virgins, in these days of wild and unsafe sex and nonchalant or irresponsible sex partners.

Options during courtship or dating: To be or not to be

At this juncture in the courtship, one has *three options* to choose from, but *only one can be chosen*:

To reinforce the relationship if it is likely to work
To improve the relationship by discussion and correction of observed lapses (if correctable)
To terminate the relationship in a decent manner, if things do not seem to be working out or nothing good is likely to materialize from it.

A costly mistake by choosing a wrong partner may earn you unhappiness for the rest of your life. So, be patient, be satisfied and take utmost care to choose your loved one, checking out *all essential elements*.

You should continuously ask yourself if you could go on to the next logical level of the relationship, provided you are ready for it. If you have even found out certain things that you do not like about your partner or cannot tolerate in a future union, you have to address the matters quickly by discussing them in a friendly manner and pointing out those areas you cannot live with. There should be no pretence about this, as your future happiness could be marred by a wrong decision.

You should therefore open your eyes and ears wide enough during courtship and before wedding, but close them as tightly as possible after you have made your choice and taken the usual, solemn vows.

Once married, remain committed and married forever. If you start to find faults with your life partner, you will continue to see them, because they are countless. So, if during courtship your partner counters or explains the fears you have voiced but you are still not satisfied, you should go ahead and break up the relationship in a nice way on grounds of incompatibility. Breaking up the relationship at this stage is far easier to handle and is less painful than breaking up a marriage (possibly with children) in future.

You should, however, still remain friendly and greet each other when you see. Do not, as a man, pretend to go on until you eat the "forbidden fruit." Apart from the time you have invested, practically nothing else has passed and you have lost nothing. In fact, you have gained some experience that can be used in future encounters with others in line for courtship or marriage. Only immature people think that unless they have had sex with girls they have moved with, they have lost. As one grows in maturity, one discovers that sex, like money, is not everything. One can move with members of the opposite sex for years and remain friendly without bringing sex into the friendship. With time, one regards such friends as blood relations and dare not ask for sexual favors. A girl in this kind of relationship will not flaunt her "assets" in such a way as to cause any arousal for the man, except she actually wants to start a relationship.

If you are rejected or "dumped" by your lover for whatever reasons, do not allow this to bother you for long. There are always many fish in the ocean. To make you forget the failed relationship quickly, you should:

1. Join a club and participate actively
2. Get a pet such as a dog or a cat to play with regularly
3. Take a vacation and enjoy yourself. In this way, you should have some time to look at the future with optimism.
4. Call and stay with friends and relations and discuss hot news of the day.
5. Exercise a lot to reduce stress
6. Go to church or a holy place to pray and thank God for his mercies
7. Tell yourself that the breakup may be a blessing in disguise for you
8. Read funny magazines and watch humorous television programs
9. Look out for a replacement if your heart tells you so

But do not smoke, drink, eat or sleep excessively, as these may worsen your plight and complicate any existing health problems.

On the other hand, if you find that you can live with your partner with all the "faults" you have found, if any, you have to go ahead and take the next logical step by getting engaged. The more you delay this step, the more faults you are likely to find. It also becomes riskier for you, as other people who have probably been waiting in the wings and praying for your failure may jump at the opportunity presented and edge you out. You may be surprised that your prospective in-laws and friends have been waiting and praying for this opportunity in this well-known game of Musical Chairs.

During this period of courtship, do not forget important dates such as birthdays and special occasions. You should send cards, flowers (where appreciated), or other gifts. Special cards with such messages as, "I love you," "You mean a lot to me," "I want you for keeps," etc., are good, but be sure you mean what you say through your actions. Action, it is said, speaks louder than voice.

Compromises and coexistence in nature

Courtship is a very important step before engagement and marriage, to ensure compatibility of couples and a long, lasting relationship or union. A man should always remember that he is a part of a woman while the latter should also remember that she is a part of a man. A man and a woman are different in various ways. Yet they have been able to stay together or coexist for hundreds of thousands (if not millions) of years without the one trying to wipe out or destroy the other. The two sexes complement, and must depend on, each other. Such natural compromises and coexistence are all around us:

Sunshine and rainfall
Positive and negative charges
Life and death
Gravity and centrifugal force
Daylight and darkness
Weak and strong nations
Rich and poor people
Fire and water
Angel and devil
Cold and Heat
Rejoicing and crying
Mountain/hill and level ground/table land
Forest and desert, etc.

Each one is important to the other and none can eliminate the other. If one could eliminate the other, then the world as we know it would not function properly, if at all. How wonderful! All of the above and more must work hand-in-hand in order for us to have a harmonious or balanced world. A good example of this harmony is the presence of trees among humans. Trees take in or breathe carbon dioxide, which humans exhale or breathe out. Humans breathe in oxygen, which trees give off or breathe out. So trees depend on animals just as animals depend on trees. Each group needs the other for survival. Another good example of this harmony is rain and sunshine. When the weather becomes unbearably hot, rain falls and cools everywhere. Sunshine is then required to dry off most of the rain and restore some balance in the surroundings again.

Highlights

After seeking out a possible future partner, you should start necessary courtship or dating. This should take *at least* six to twelve months.

Find out every important detail about your future partner.

Be truthful and faithful and nurture the relationship in various ways.

Then finally decide if you want to go ahead with, or breakup, the relationship.

If you have to breakup, do so without looking back, but be *nice* about it.

If you have to go ahead, do so with dispatch and get formally engaged.

Chapter 4

Formal Engagement

"Tell the whole world that you have found a future partner."

Dangers of trial marriage

The period of courtship enables two intending partners, friends, or mates, to find out much about each other. It is always a two-way street. Courtship may be short or long, depending on what one would like to accomplish before engagement or marriage. A very long courtship is not encouraged, as there is always the danger that one of the parties may "derail" when temptation comes knocking. A party can always pull out of a relationship for reasons as varied as the number of people involved.

No one is ever completely satisfied with a chosen partner in all relevant respects. It is generally everyone's ambition to have a partner who has all usually desirable qualities such as good family background, sound education, beautiful and athletic body, prosperous job or business, good character, etc. You may dream there is someone out there who is better in some respects, which may prompt you to make a change for the "last time." Chances are if you keep changing your partner as you change your clothes, you may never get married or be seriously committed. A rolling stone, as the saying goes, gathers no moss.

In the same way, a very short courtship is to be discouraged, as both lovers are not likely to find out a lot about each other during this time. Background checks are therefore equally important. Lovers require some time to study each other and obtain useful information before falling head over heals—at which time they have reached the point of no return.

In this regard, lovers sometimes may be tempted to resort to "trial marriage" for some time to enable them find out if they are compatible partners. A trial mar-

30

riage involves lovers living under the same roof and doing virtually "everything" that a truly married couple does, before being properly recognized as husband and wife by society. Thus, the liaison is illegal and at the same time immoral, even though the intentions may be good. This should never be resorted to, as it easily exposes practising lovers to various weaknesses. The relationship usually ends acrimoniously, destroying possible future plans and throwing up negative attitudes toward the opposite sex. Parents should not approve or tolerate this kind of relationship. Rather, regular exchange of visits by both lovers should be encouraged. The female involved usually has more to lose than the male, before the eyes of the world. Serious emotional disturbance could result from being suddenly thrown into the streets or back to her parents' house. There is thus no such thing as a "trial marriage" in the eyes of the law or various religions or society as a whole. Those engaging in it do so at their own risk. It could also lead to a palimony case, to the detriment of the "pals" who lived together like husband and wife but were unmarried under an oral contract or memorandum of understanding.

Popping the question

Engagement and marriage should be taken seriously, as your success or failure in life may very well depend on this. There should, however, be no turning back once your mind is made up. ***But each step you take must follow logically from the one before***. It is assumed that up to this point in time your mind has been made up, that you like and love your partner in all respects and that there is no turning back.

You should now as a man, in your privacy with her, *formally* pop the question she has been waiting for all this time, in these or similar words: "My darling, will you marry me? I love you with all my heart." Then slip the engagement ring into her hand or, as some would prefer to do, put it in a special pack and give it to her. An embrace and a long passionate kiss could follow a "yes" answer. Celebrations to mark the occasion may follow, or there may be no celebrations at all, making it more or less very informal and private.

Surprisingly, a "no" answer could be given, in which case you have to start all over again to look for your future partner. It should be understood that good lovers do not necessarily make good husbands and wives. On the other hand, acrimonious lovers could make good husbands and wives once they become committed, so a disappointed man should take it with equanimity. Reasons for the "no" answer could be sought, if you have the heart, to guide you in your future search. This is like learning from your mistakes, if any. Perhaps, with the benefit of hindsight, you may one day discover that the disappointment was a blessing in disguise.

Sometimes, too, disappointment comes from the man who develops "cold feet" at the eleventh hour. He should then search for suitable words and circumstances to explain his actions to his erstwhile lover, while hoping for forgiveness and eventual healing of wounds. Mending a broken heart is not always easy.

31

Informing friends and relations

Next, parents, relations, and possibly friends should be informed of these new developments, except they were present during the celebrations marking the engagement. Since both partners have consented to get married, approval from these relations, including their blessings, is a mere formality.

Eloping with a loved one on the grounds of family disapproval will not help either party, as you will still come back to your family at a point in future. Rather, continue to appeal (and explain your reasons) to opposing family members, who may yield after some time. Where opposition is still great, you should then decide whether it is in your own interest to go it alone or not. Follow legal and customary practices in your locality in all of the above to ensure you do not step on someone's toes or run foul of applicable laws. Be as modest as possible in spending money to avoid borrowing. Do not let your happy mood make you say "yes" to unreasonable or unnecessary expenses. Suggestions for these extras can be declined politely or humorously.

Men should actually be reminded that it is women who make the choice when they say "yes." Men propose while it is up to women to accept or reject. This is similar to "offer" and "acceptance" in the law of contract. These days, there may be some conditions attached to the acceptance. Men should not force women against their wishes, just as in sexual relations, if they are to avoid being charged with rape and/or abduction. No doubt, a woman's wish is sometimes difficult to determine. Some say "yes" but don't actually mean it, while some say "no" and may mean "yes." Sometimes, it is difficult to know if "yes" or "no" is meant. It is characteristic of women to be *equivocal* in sexual matters. But that's the name of the game. Many people, including celebrities, can tell you their experiences with women who visited them. These women apparently made suggestive or seductive moves and perhaps acquiesced in the men's romantic behaviors or moves, leading the men to have sex with them. However, these women charged the men with *rape* afterwards and won, even after so many months following the encounter. With luck on a man's side, correct judgment may be made as to whether a woman has agreed to have sex or not. But even if she changes her mind during a sexual encounter, the man must stop or "come down" or dismount immediately, to avoid being charged with rape. In many countries, particularly Western nations, it does not matter if a man is the husband or has had a long-term sexual relationship. It is also no excuse that the man has reached the "point of no return," whatever this means outside a medical and legal definition. Perhaps it is the time a man reaches the highest point of ecstasy when having sex. It has been a tricky game at best. So, men must be careful and avoid going to jail for a momentary enjoyment. It is not worth the trouble and humiliation. In virtually all countries of the world, men welcome ladies touching any parts of their bodies, even their private parts, without explicit permission. Men hardly complain. Even if those sensitive parts were touched inadvertently and the ladies apologized, men would jokingly tell them not to apologize because they enjoyed it. However, the same thing cannot be said of many ladies who, when caught red-handed, can easily deny any consensual sex or granting permission to touch their bodies and may raise rape charges. Men should therefore learn how to read ladies' lips and minds together in order to avoid any trouble. Whatever is good does not come cheap.

In the lower animal kingdom, females also make the choice by looking for the best among competing and horn-locking or fighting males. In many situations, males lure females by making beautiful nests or homes for them, tonguing them all over, displaying colorful feathers, following them for days, providing some food, and passing other "tests" as tacitly demanded by females before the latter yield to male sexual overtures. Sometimes, this courtship may last from a few hours to as long as a full month.

Incidentally, human behavior is not different. Men lure women with power, money, cars, houses, dresses, high-class food, holidays in exotic places, jewelry and elaborate courtship, among other lures. Powerful positions on the corporate ladder or in government, social status and background, future prospects, and other material or exotic things that are valued by women, based on their stations in life and social circumstances, are also used by men to lure them.

Some women also test men's patience, seriousness and ability to protect them against dangers and other changing circumstances of life before accepting them as sexual or lifetime partners.

There is no doubt that during courtship some family members or friends might have noticed both partners and their movements. Some of them might have asked a few searching questions, particularly mothers in their anxiety to ensure that "nothing but the best" was good for their children. "Elders" at a point during courtship might have given a few words of advice or caution, all pointing to the need for partners to be careful in making their choice and not rush matters. Appropriately, such remarks or questions as these might have been used or asked:

"I hope he/she is from a good home. Have you checked?"
"Why not wait a few more years? Why are you in such a hurry?"
"I hope you have thought the matter over and over again."
"Why not wait until she first becomes pregnant, so as to be sure she is not barren?"
"Can you handle a man/woman well? You are too young."

All these questions and remarks are usually well taken because everyone wants the marriage to succeed through happy, fruitful, and long-lasting relationship.

Advice from elders or senior citizens is important and should be taken seriously. Many a time, young people, in a haste to get married, do not see from a standing and near position what elders see from a sitting and distant position. Elders have the benefit of hindsight and foresight and should be listened to.

A formal engagement is an announcement to the "whole world" (local areas involved) that partners or lovers are now serious about getting married after a long courtship. It is also a form of unsolicited advice or warning that all other interested parties should steer clear, particularly of the female. This is why an engagement must be taken seriously. Partners have now "arrived" to take on an important responsibility in life. Very soon, assuming everything works out well, they will become parents to be looked up to by their children for everything.

Some engagement practices worldwide and the need to follow local practices/laws

In some parts of the world, particularly *Africa*, if a man makes up his mind about a partner, he formally informs his family members at a special meeting that has been scheduled for the purpose. They then appoint a "linkman," "middle-man," or "errand man" for the intending bridegroom. Such a linkman must be quite knowledgeable about marriage customs and rites to enable him perform relevant tasks effectively. His main duty is to discuss with the man seeking a wife and his prospective in-laws and obtain details of everything that is required by the in-laws. He interacts with the latter from time to time or as dictated by circumstances. Any expenses incurred by him in performing these assignments are payable or refundable by the prospective bridegroom. He finally arranges a *full meeting* with members of the girl's family. Both families will obtain a full "dossier" about themselves, to enable them bless or oppose the proposed union or even place some conditions such as requiring the couple to wed in the church or registry and in training some relations of the girl.

The bridegroom's relations take assorted drinks, "kola-nuts" and other items (such as clothing, food, trinkets, etc.) to the in-laws for the introductory discussion leading to marriage.

Of course, there are variations here and there as you move from one locality to another and, as you may have rightly guessed, from one country to another.

All in all, the idea behind this meeting is to get acquainted with in-laws on both sides and cement the relationship.

At the gathering as prearranged, after exchange of greetings and pleasantries with a lot of jokes, the hosts first introduce themselves and offer kola-nuts and drinks to welcome their guests. Then the visitors from the man's side follow, offering drinks and kola-nuts and stating the reason for their visit, even though this is known in advance. As the discussion progresses (with appropriate jokes and parables here and there), the girl is called out by her relations to confirm that she would like to marry the man. This confirmation usually takes the form of drinking from the same cup or glass which her lover or prospective husband has used; in fact, the lover actually leaves some drink for the girl to finish, thus confirming their closeness. Again, there are variations here and there, the idea being to confirm that they are in love and have accepted to be husband and wife.

Expectedly, the "yes" answer will now take both sides into serious negotiations in connection with dowry payment by the man. If the discussion turns out well (sometimes lasting eight to twelve hours or even overnight), the man settles a part of the dowry on the spot by *cash payment* (not check, money order, IOU, or credit/debit card). This is reminiscent of the era when dowry was settled with goats, cattle, other domestic animals, cowries, or other exchange media which could be shared on the spot by the bridegroom's in-laws. Foreign currencies such as the U.S. dollar or British pound sterling are now sometimes used in some places where local currencies lose value quickly. A good thing about dowry payment is that it can be partially settled and, in many instances, it may never be fully paid. In this way, the line of communication between the man and his in-laws remains open for a long time, thus further cementing the relationship. Creditworthiness does not apply here as if one were going to buy a car or obtain a loan. If a prospective bridegroom is deemed financially weak by his family members, the latter come to his support from behind the scene. Establishing good relationship between in-laws is what matters most.

Thereafter, elders bless both the man and the woman. They are also given words of advice. Sometimes, some elders may chip in some jovial words of advice and prayers such as: "May conception take place after only one sexual encounter! May the good Lord give you the means or resources for bringing up your children! By the way, we do not count our children, the more the merrier."

Those present laugh uncontrollably at such funny remarks. Great rejoicing, eating, drinking and dancing usually follow. The girl's family then serves food to everyone. *In the eyes of all present, the man and woman are now husband and wife.* For such customary marriages, no marriage certificates are issued and there is no signing over dotted lines. But all present are witnesses to the events and can be summoned in future to testify if any problems arise. Some of these practices, which have been handed down over time, are reminiscent of ancient times when people were illiterate and did not keep records, apart from oral tradition.

Finally, a date is fixed when the bride will be formally escorted to the bridegroom's home. This ceremony is also very elaborate as the girl virtually picks up every article that will be useful in her new home. These items include clothes, boxes, cooking utensils, mortar and pestle, sewing machine, trinkets, shoes, etc. Her parents and well-to-do relations usually provide most of the items. Very rich families provide expensive articles, to show off their affluence.

In the meantime, while the bridegroom and his relations are on their way home, the other side gathers in the house of the oldest man among them to share the dowry (as specified by custom) and consume any leftovers—food or drinks.

The involvement of relations in engagement and dowry negotiations tends to bring stability and respectability in marital relations. It also emphasizes the dependence of one side on the other and vice versa. After all, the two have become "one flesh" and should be seen as one. In this connection, a husband cannot simply throw out his wife or try to harm her in any way without first thinking of the consequences of his action among his in-laws and their possible reactions. The same thing can be said about the wife who cannot take any unilateral action against her husband without some support from her relations and appropriate notice to her in-laws through her elders. What this means in effect is that when a husband gravely offends his wife by having other serious relationships or neglecting her welfare, she is entitled to report the matter to her relations and in-laws.

They must try to reconcile both husband and wife and restore peace and love to their home. In the same way, when a wife offends her husband, the latter is supposed to report the matter to his in-laws and relations for their intervention. If the matter is grave, bordering on infidelity on the part of the wife, she is immediately "suspended" from cooking for her husband until she "cleanses" herself and undergoes all necessary rituals, supervised by her husband's elderly female relations. This is done if the husband still wants back his wife; otherwise the cleansing is unnecessary. Thus, marriage is seen as a responsibility for all relations and in-laws.

However, affairs or illegal sexual liaisons by husbands are only punished if they involve the wives of relations or very close female relations. Even distant cousins are regarded as close relations and any affairs with them are considered taboo and equally punished.

In some Western societies such as Canada, USA, Australia and European countries that have similar customs, etc, engagement ceremonies are far less formal or elaborate than has been presented above. After courtship, which may or may not be long, the man proposes to the woman when they are alone, usually in a half-kneeling position.

He may say something like this: "Darling, I have loved you for so long and would like you to be with me the rest of my life. Will you marry me?" If "yes" is the answer, the man places a fairly expensive engagement ring in her finger. He then seals the memorable event with a good, passionate and long kiss. How easy and quick! Friends or relations may or may not be invited and the simple ceremony may be in the man's or girl's home or over candlelight dinner. Where celebrities are involved, the engagement may take a more formal outlook, characterized by special drinks, such as champagne, and a few speeches.

Still, in some societies, an engagement ceremony is formalized by "heavy" entertainment with food, drink, and dancing. Parents of the bride usually receive accolades for successfully bringing up their daughter, without teenage pregnancy and other problems associated with bringing up girls.

Whatever culture you find yourself in, you should know your in-laws through formal introductions.

If you think it is only the lower animals that lock horns when it comes to mating or looking for a partner, you are wrong. In some primitive cultures even today, men who want to marry slug it out through wrestling matches. The winner in a particular match is then entitled to marry a lady that is ripe for marriage. Still in some cultures, an intending bridegroom is subjected to painful floggings with horse whips to test his endurance and thus his ability to withstand the strains or problems of marriage.

The way engagement is done, as has been said previously, varies from culture to culture. Each culture thinks theirs is the best because they are used to it and have practised it for long.

Sexual relations (or anticipation of sex) thereafter

What then is next after engagement? Should the man and woman start living together? Should they now engage in sexual relations? The best advice in this circumstance is for the two to agree on what is best for them, with the man leading the discussion. If they agree (tacitly or expressly) to have immediate sexual relations, this is fine, but they should be aware of the consequences of any resulting pregnancy. If one of them supports and the other opposes, it is better for them to wait until after a formal wedding, if it is just a couple of weeks away. Sometimes, this kind of decision is not easy to make where one of the parties is going to be away for a long time, say six months or more. Why should they not consummate this union before the temporary parting of ways? After all, they have waited for a long time. However, let the couple decide for themselves, taking adequate and healthy precautions if thought necessary in the circumstance.

It should also be mentioned that some cultures permit lovemaking and living together after a formal engagement as a way of testing partners' compatibility or introducing them to what is ahead. But some families discourage this practice until the dotted lines are signed.

However, all this "puritanism" is gradually breaking down. More and more ladies are signing the dotted lines with protruding stomachs. Priests may not like this development as it infringes on the Christian principle of "no sex before wedding," but at least this situation is better than having an abortion performed, just to appear to be pure or chaste on the wedding day, when the opposite is the case. It is choosing the lesser of two evils.

With the engagement ceremony over, the couple should be seen more and more together. Should the now-engaged couple move to newer heights by a formal marriage, however celebrated? If "yes," then preparations should begin in earnest. Planning, as in business, ensures that there are no serious omissions and that expenses as projected can be borne by the couple, their families and friends. If not, activities should be reduced to a level that is affordable by the couple and consistent with the prevailing mood in the locality.

Highlights

You, the man, should make a formal proposal to your loved one, choosing an appropriate venue and time.

Follow up with introduction to in-laws and relations on both sides.

Perform all the rites required to formalize the engagement, including settling dowry price where required.

Decide whether to start living together and having sexual relations. Weigh the consequences carefully.

Start planning for a formal wedding, if you want one. If not, both of you can start living together as husband and wife.

Chapter 5

Preparations for Wedding

"Cut your coat according to your size and cloth."

Prenuptial counseling

A very important step after engagement is attending pre-wedding counseling sessions. Each couple is advised to find time to attend. These sessions are usually arranged by some churches, professional counselors and other groups for intending couples. In many organizations, these sessions are *mandatory* before wedding takes place. What is usually discussed during these sessions includes, but is not limited to:

Mentioning possible problem areas during marriage and how to avoid or solve them

Learning from the mistakes of others, in order to strengthen a marriage

Learning to appreciate each other and recognize that each person has weaknesses with which a couple must live. Each person also has contributions to make while married, in order to make it successful.

Reminding a couple of their responsibilities toward each other and their children, who must be brought up in a loving atmosphere. They also have responsibilities toward their in-laws and friends and the greater society as a whole.

Having the opportunity to voice out concerns and fears and having necessary reassurances and advice from professionals in the field.

Other matters of interest to a couple, such as making preparations for the actual wedding and, perhaps, the need to be prudent in spending.

It is also the last opportunity for a couple to test their love and finally make up their minds on whether to proceed or not. The sessions are rewarding and should not be missed, particularly as they present an opportunity to meet other intending couples and enjoy a lot of jokes during the sessions.

Level of preparation: Time, money and mood

Should you engage in outward and sometimes expensive ceremonies to solemnize your marriage, including the social events that follow? Should these be limited and so be less expensive, thus saving money for trying times in future? Who should be invited to these ceremonies and socials? Who should be left out and why? Should it be a church wedding or a simple registry/court wedding or even a simple "native wedding"? Should all food items and drinks be farmed out or should relations and friends assist in getting these prepared? Will the wedding dress be specially designed and sewn by, or purchased from, exclusive shops in London, Paris, New York, Los Angeles, Rome, Tokyo, Abidjan, Hong Kong, Shanghai, Honolulu, Bombay, Las Vegas, Lagos, Johannesburg, or Rio de Janeiro? How many flower girls and pageboys will be needed? Where will the reception take place—Hilton, Western, Ramada, Sheraton, Federal Palace, Airport Hotel, Eko, Wardolf Astoria, or a local club?

These and similar questions usually bother those preparing for their wedding. The anxieties are natural, as well as the urge to have a successful marriage outing. Getting married used to be done *once* in one's lifetime. These days, some people seem heartless where love is concerned and have been known to change partners up to eight or more times in their lifetime, for very flimsy reasons.

The answers to these questions are not easy. No one has all the answers, but you should be ready to accept compromise solutions in the interest of all. Above all, *availability of time and material resources* is likely to be the determining factor if a major wedding is being planned.

Both the man and the woman have crucial roles to play to ensure reasonable success. In the end, you will discover that what matters in a marriage is not these outward performances but true love for each other. Without this, the marriage may not last. True love will push them to make necessary sacrifices by subordinating their personal interests to those of the family as a single unit.

If you go through the history of major weddings involving kings, princes, rich people, and other celebrities, you will find that not many of the weddings survived the test of time. Were outward performances and heavy expenditure the sole criterion for success, these weddings would be successes. On the contrary, go through the history of the weddings of lesser mortals and other less privileged people, and you will be surprised to see how successful the couples have been, notwithstanding their relative poverty. So, money or riches or influential background should never be a major consideration in choosing a partner or in preparing for a wedding. People still celebrate happily, even in poverty.

Recall the *soliloquy* of the king in William Shakespeare's play, <u>Henry V</u>, where he lamented the relative unhappiness of a king (with all the opulence around him) as compared with the position of peasants or poor people who seemed relatively happy and carefree in their poverty. Presence of real love, the ability to give and take, humility, tolerance, patience, and responsibility are some of the qualities or key issues that should be favorably considered. As the old saying goes, "Cut your coat according to your size." To this, one may hasten to add: "And according to the actual quantity of cloth available or affordable."

Prenuptial agreements and weird provisions

A new trend in the last couple of years has been the signing of a **prenuptial agreement** specifying what each party should obtain or pay to the disadvantaged or aggrieved party on breakup of a marriage. This, to say the least, is in very bad taste. This is so because both parties, even before its actual occurrence, are already *con - templating* that the marriage will fail. Contemplation of failure is as bad as actual failure itself and is self-defeating and borders on pessimism. Such a marriage, it must be said, is devoid of real love and a good foundation. Rather, it concerns itself with material things or wealth and assumes that marriage is to be treated like a business venture in which one tries to maximize gains while minimizing or eliminating losses. Prenuptial agreements are usually signed within rich circles. A poor man or woman has little or no valuable property to protect or lose, even in the event of a divorce. The only thing lost, perhaps, is the love of the ex-partner.

As regards prenuptial agreements, consider this scenario. A clever partner who never really loved the mate can fake love, enter into a prenuptial agreement and formally get married. As soon as any opportunity for divorce presents itself, the unscrupulous partner seizes it and falls back on the prenuptial agreement. Perhaps you may not blame anybody for this development in today's relationships. Like the proverbial bird that refuses to perch to avoid sharp shooting humans, men and women have learned to protect themselves in an increasingly uncertain and volatile world of marriages or what looks like marriages. No one wants to be caught unaware or lose so much money and properties these days to an ex-partner. As the apt saying goes, "To be *forewarned is to be forearmed.*"

To some people therefore, having a prenuptial agreement in place is one way of arming themselves against any contingency such as divorce. To others, having God and good people around them, as well as good intentions, will be all they need.

Some rich men usually favor prenuptial agreements. This is perhaps borne out of experience from previous court divorce settlements, which nearly crippled those involved financially. Some women, too, not to be outdone (for fear of being used and thrown out with nothing by unscrupulous men), ask for prenuptial agreements under which they are able to get something with which to start life again in the event of a divorce. Only God knows whether monetary compensation helps to heal such wounds or not. Money, as has been proven time and time again, does not seem to make people happier or live longer. As long as their basic needs have been met, poor people will surely feel happy and perhaps live to ripe, old age. Generally, on the other hand, rich or well-to-do people eat a lot, drink a lot, and laze around a lot. In the process, they take ill and may die young.

In some instances, prenuptial agreements have even gone "nuclear" and have been expanded beyond reasonable expectations. They include such laughable or ridiculous provisions as the number of times sex can be had in a month or week, who is to pay for what, and who is to take children to school and bring them back. Other provisions relate to the number of children they will have, whether relations are to visit and what programs to watch on television. These provisions may sound bizarre, but they have been included in prenuptial agreements. You can then begin to see the worthlessness of prenuptial agreements.

Will you go to court each time there is actual or perceived breach of any of the provisions? What will happen if one of the partners refuses or is unable or unwilling to participate effectively during a sexual encounter as provided for in the agreement? How can this lapse or breach be presented in court or even replayed before a jury for purposes of determining the guilt or innocence of either party? In the absence of any witnesses (there are usually none in sexual encounters except God), whose story will be believed, his or hers? This may require a Solomon-like decision. The time, money, and effort wasted on this kind of matter are better imagined than spent.

A couple should never (in their individual capacity) contemplate gains or losses from marriage. These are supposed to accrue to the couple together as a single unit or entity. *Gains or losses are for both parties,* as the two are now one flesh. No one should make a profit at the expense of the other. Why should one rob Peter in order to pay Paul?

List of possible activities and responsibilities

So, the level of preparation depends on the pocket, time available, the mood of the celebrants and other extraneous factors. Activities that can be farmed out and better handled by outsiders should be so treated, with a careful note of the names and addresses of contractors, quantities, amounts, delivery points, and dates. In short, *all activities contemplated* should be listed in an orderly manner, discussed with friends and relations (for their advice) before decisions are reached as to what to do. A possible *checklist* is suggested below:

Date and time of wedding
Place of wedding (church, registry, mosque, synagogue, etc.)
Sponsors or witnesses and addresses
Chief bridesmaid (or maid of honor), bridesmaids, and addresses
Flowergirls, ringbearers and addresses
Bestman, bridegroom's men, and addresses
Wedding rings
Printing of invitation cards and invitees: parents, in-laws, business associates, relations, friends, classmates, etc.
Prayers, songs and arrangement with the choir/rehearsal with officiating minister
Preparations of reception hall, and address of the decorator
Wedding cake and address of maker

Master of ceremonies and his assistants

High table sitting arrangement/Chairman for the occasion (except it will be an informal reception)

Food, snacks, plates, and cutlery

Drinks, glasses, and tissue/cleaning paper

Music and address of DJ

Helpers and assistants at reception

Photographs and addresses of photographers

Distribution of invitation cards

Toast proposals

Gifts and care over them

Wedding dress for the bride and address of seamstress and fitters

Wedding suit or dress for the bridegroom

Dresses for others—cost to be borne by them or by couple

Transportation to and from various venues for special people

Clearing of reception hall after social ceremony

It is a good idea to check off each activity as it is discussed and finalized. Follow up from time to time, possibly through telephone calls, to ensure everything is on course. Reminders in writing will assist helpers a lot, lest they forget. The couple should decide how each activity is to be financed or taken care of by each of them, with the assistance of relations and friends if they are lucky. If finances are likely to run out, the couple should roll back some activities and cut down the number of invitees. Remember that a wedding can be had with only the witnesses, parents, and a few close friends. Do not try to impress anybody, as you have your own lives to live later and no one may come to your assistance then. So check your pockets very well before embarking on a princely wedding, if both of you are middle-class workers or low-income earners. An elephant should carry an amount of load relative to its size. An antelope should not take on any luggage meant for an elephant; otherwise it may collapse under the weight. Therefore, cut your coat not only according to your size but also according to the quantity of cloth actually available.

Remember, too, that all arrangements can never be one hundred per cent perfect, even if you have so many years to prepare for the wedding. Learn, therefore, to *keep your cool and do some tradeoffs.*

Where no social ceremony or formal wedding is contemplated, you are free to start living together with your partner and sharing the responsibilities and pleasures of marriage. However, since marriage is contemplated only once in a lifetime (except you are among some Hollywood stars and celebrities who are free to change partners as many times as they want and even break up other people's marriages), you should try to make it as memorable as possible in your own special way, for posterity. This does not necessarily mean extravagance.

Visit to wedding and reception venues

To give a couple more confidence on the wedding day, it may be a good idea for them to visit the wedding and reception venues at least once, to practise movements, know the exact entry points, see seating positions, and learn its general layout. They should find out, too, if they need to see the priest, pastor, rabbi, or alpha in advance to iron out important issues and to ensure that all replies to inquiries have been received by him. If you are required to read portions of the Bible or any other holy book during service, you should go over those portions at home. In so doing, you gain necessary confidence and avoid stumbling over difficult words in the full glare of those attending.

As regards wedding venues, it is not uncommon for some couples in special professions or vocations to choose what many would consider weird venues such as tree tops, fire trucks, ships, water, a trampoline, and even garbage dumps, with officiating ministers in attendance. One couple even insisted on being driven to the garbage dump venue in a garbage truck. Other weird wedding matters include wearing a special dress that looks like scarecrow. Others wear work uniforms, military uniforms (which may be okay for members of the armed forces), swim trunks, or simply appear in their "birthday suit." As regards the latter, there are reports of couples who decide to go completely naked for wedding ceremonies in secluded locations, with their guests also agreeing to go naked, along with officiating ministers. All these point to extreme behaviors in societies where many people do not know what to do with their abundant freedom. Many people may start to ask if all is well with such couples. So going so far from what is ordinary or normal may raise eyebrows. The erstwhile respect such couples had with friends and relations may soon disappear.

Bachelor's night

For intending couples, bachelor's night and spinster's night are important. While their friends make all the arrangements, they should ensure that they do not drink on this occasion. In fact, they should not spend more than one hour while hobnobbing with their single friends. They need a lot of rest, while their friends and relations help them to supervise various activities. They should not try to do everything themselves, as they could break down, particularly if the woman is pregnant.

Time won't be anybody's friend now. Couples need at least six hours of sleep on their wedding eve, so as to be properly relaxed for the joyous occasion ahead. Anything less may make them nervous and agitated.

Highlights

Check your pocket and decide the level of wedding required.
List all activities required and people responsible for them
Follow up regularly to ensure everything is on course.

A prenuptial agreement does not guarantee the success of a marriage; rather a quick breakup is contemplated, making the marriage a failure <u>ab initio</u> (from the beginning).

Do not do anything to impress others; feel satisfied with whatever you can afford.

Bachelor's/spinster's night should be short, as you need a lot of rest for the next day's event.

Chapter 6
Formal Wedding Ceremony

"Make your wedding day the happiest time in your life."

Time and punctuality

The day is like any other day, except for many anxieties. The last two to three days might have been spent without any sleep at all, simply to ensure that all arrangements would work out fine. It is for this reason that some couples usually arrange to take some days from their jobs at this time. This is highly recommended. All the same, even if one year is taken to prepare for a wedding, time may still appear to be short as the long expected day draws nearer and nearer.

If all arrangements for a formal wedding have been taken care of reasonably well, then it is a mere formality to go to church, mosque, synagogue, or registry. There, the usual vows of faithfulness to, and care and love for, each other, under constantly changing conditions "until death comes calling," are taken.

Perhaps, the most important thing for you to do on the wedding day is to have your eyes on the clock and ensure that you have at least fifteen minutes to settle down when you get to the venue. On that day, the main enemy is time. No one can draw the hands of the clock backwards. Ceremonies have had to be held up simply because one of the parties failed to show up promptly. Even in some instances, one of the partners had backed off at the eleventh hour without the courtesy of informing the mate until it was too late. The consequent embarrassment to the partner, relations, clergy, friends and all those assembled is better imagined than experienced. This kind of behavior is rather childish and should be condemned in clear terms. There is no doubt that stage fright can be mainly responsible for such a behavior. Perhaps, one partner wants to retaliate openly for the other partner's "misdemeanor" or "felony" during the period of courtship. It is possible that a non-palatable story has just reached the deserter, who then decides to withdraw rather than be committed for life and thereafter regret the relationship.

A couple should have their eyes on the clock (with the assistance of helpers around, particularly as regards the bride, who has so many dresses to wear and so much makeup to use). A reasonable allowance should be made for traffic delays. There should be no problem reaching the venue of the ceremony slightly ahead of schedule. This should be aimed at so that a couple does not become the subject of gossips when they eventually arrive. This will also ensure that no serious pressure builds up in them should they start to run late. The bride usually outshines the bridegroom on a day like this. All eyes are focused on her, some in total admiration for her beauty and poise, and some in contempt, perhaps for the size or flamboyance of the wedding dress. If all those who have roles to play at the ceremony are present, it should be over within ninety minutes. Church or other ceremonies vary from place to place. The bride and bridegroom may be required to participate actively by reading from the Bible or other holy books. From time to time, they may be required by the officiating minister to get up for some ceremonies, with the chief bridesmaid and the bestman by their sides. In the end, what matters is that they have exchanged sacred vows and rings, promising, among other matters, to love each other in sickness and in health ... "until death do us part."

Biblical injunctions

If it is a Christian wedding, one of the readings may include quotations from St. Paul's Epistle to the Ephesians exhorting a husband to love his wife and the latter to obey her husband. The qualities of a good wife may also be mentioned, as well as the dangerous anger that flows from the husband of an adulterous wife. For many Christians and some adherents of other religions, the vows of marriage before God's "instrument" or "representative" seal the wedding, which becomes indissoluble in some religions. Remember the Lord Jesus Christ's injunction:

What God has joined together, let no man put asunder!

This injunction is one of the various pronouncements of our Lord Jesus Christ on marriage and divorce, as given in Matthew 19:3-12. For those who think that they can throw out their partners like dirt or garbage, they should absorb what our Lord Jesus advised:

...And I say to you, whoever divorces his wife, except for sexual immorality, and marries another, commits adultery; and whoever marries her who is divorced commits adultery.

I hope Hollywood stars and other celebrities have read this portion of the Bible, or they think it is irrelevant as far as their lives are concerned, since the world revolves around them.

The interpretation of this injunction, in my humble opinion, is that a man can divorce his wife only on grounds of sexual immorality, if she has affairs or sleeps with any one other than her husband. Now, what of the wife? Can she divorce her husband on any grounds at all? No direction or clear-cut answer is available from the Bible except as may be inferred from our Lord's injunction given above, which, apparently, means "no." Does this therefore mean that a woman has no grounds or rights whatsoever to divorce her husband under any circumstances? It is difficult to make any clear-cut pronouncements on this question.

You may shout "discrimination" but how else can this assertion not be positively supported? Read that portion of the Bible again. Even where sexual immorality as indicated by our Lord is involved, many religions find it difficult to grant divorce to couples, preferring instead to reconcile them by asking innocent spouses to forgive erring partners. No doubt, this approach helps to stabilize marriages. It also makes couples learn from their mistakes and respect the feelings of their spouses.

Struggle between monogamy and polygamy

Men, but not women, by their nature are polygamous. This is supported by facts from history and even from the Bible and by what happens in the lower animal kingdom. Here a male may keep as many females as possible and defend his territory and the females therein against other male intruders, even to the death. A man may be a higher animal biologically and socially, but he is not much different from his relatives in the lower animal kingdom, both having apparently evolved from the same roots. Women, too, by nature, have always looked up to men for protection and care and have tolerated (if not totally accepted) polygamous relationships. In some cultures of Africa, it is even the most "senior wives" who select (or approve) more wives for their husbands as soon as the latter indicate their intention to have more wives under native law and custom, as dictated by economic and other circumstances. The main reason for this approach is that the senior wives must ensure that they can live in harmony with the new wives. This was also generally so even in the Western world until church doctrines, civil laws and economic realities gradually changed all that to what are now popular and almost standard today—monogamous relationships.

But in the *Moslem world* (where Islam permits four wives, if the husband can maintain them) and some other parts of the world, polygamous marriages have hardly died down, even though many western-minded women are beginning to abhor such practices. The Holy Koran, which was written or revealed in the seventh century when men were apparently scarce due principally to deaths in wars, specifically permits up to four wives for a man under certain conditions. However, in modern times, many Moslem countries such as Turkey and Tunisia have banned polygamy outright, while others such as Indonesia have sought to make it mandatory for the first wife to approve her husband's request to marry additional wives. Women, on their part, due to improved education, information, and universal civil rights, have been seeking to make it easier for them to have divorce from their husbands who may want to marry extra wives. Thus, Moslem women, like their Western counterparts, now feel it is their right to have only one love or husband whom they do not wish to share with other women in the name of religion. There are many and varied opinions on the strict interpretation of the Holy Koran on this issue. The matter will be the subject of a prolonged debate between conservatives and moderates in the years to come. Perhaps, like their Western counterparts, clever or outgoing Moslem men could marry one wife officially but maintain a bevy of girl friends or mistresses.

However, in many royal families where money and power reign supreme, many women may not mind being in a polygamous setting. Thus, as long as both men and women love the setting, polygamy may not die down so soon. Many women on their part, instead of remaining single, would rather be second, third, or fourth wives. When they answer "Mrs. Whatever-it-is," nobody will know that they are second, third, or fourth wives, except they are told. At least this setting makes them happier than remaining single.

Even in the *Christian world* where monogamy is supposed to be the order of the day, some married men go out of their way to keep girlfriends or mistresses and pretend they are pious until they are exposed. Only those caught are the real "villains." People then shout "Scandal!" This, all the same, has not stopped people, particularly men, from being what nature has made them to be. The struggle between monogamy, with sanctimonious behavior, and polygamous or multiple relationships is heating up. Both sides enjoy their positions. A *monogamist* may say "I cannot afford to maintain any relationship outside my marriage. Let me keep what I have. I am satisfied." On the other hand, a *polygamist* may say "I have a lot of time and resources at my disposal. Let me enjoy myself by having multiple partners or wives, as life is too short." There may never be a clear winner, but the struggle certainly continues. Thus, for a majority of men, every nice looking woman is on their "wish list" for sex, because they see their actions as boosting their egos. The same thing cannot be said of women, who, by and large, prefer one relationship at a time, unlike men who practise multiple relationships just to enjoy sex and brag about their "conquests." This behavior on the part of men does not necessarily mean that they do not love their wives. They do love them and will jealously protect them from other men. But all this behavior comes with a price or cost, many a time very unpleasant and high, as compared with the momentary sexual encounter.

Sexual revolution and assumed freedoms

Due to the high level of lust and materialistic trends in today's society, however, righteous behavior appears to be losing out. What is more, society encourages this by drumming it in everybody's ears that freedom includes sexual freedom in all its ramifications, as soon as the age of eighteen years is attained.

Here goes:

Freedom to date or keep friends of the opposite sex for sexual or amorous relationships

Freedom to wear any kind of skimpy dress that virtually exposes all private parts of the body, leaving nothing to the imagination anymore.

Freedom to use any kind of contraceptives.

Freedom to abort pregnancies, even in the sixth month and upwards.

Freedom to practise any forms of sexual relationships including _homosexuality_, and to perform any sexual acts as an entertainment before a live and appreciative audience. It may not be surprising if the law in future permits people to perform incestuous acts, all in the name of freedom

Freedom to marry or not to marry and to have children, within or outside a marriage

Freedom to change one's sex and to change again and again at any time, sometimes at cost to other members of society who are "straight"

Freedom to dress much like members of the opposite sex, with some men wearing earrings, plaited or braided hair, and lipstick and with some women not wearing any of these anymore and even wearing hairstyles traditionally meant for men. This makes it difficult sometimes to distinguish between a man and a woman, except through extensive, medical examination, complete with DNA and other sophisticated tests. Look around and see how difficult it is to tell a man apart from a woman. To make matters worse, men perform jobs traditionally meant for women and vice versa. Where do we draw the line in these days of sexual freedom and equality? Who will draw the line?

Freedom for men to answer exclusively female names and vice versa for women.

Freedom to divorce and remarry as many times as possible.

Freedom to break up other people's marriages, all in the name of love.

Freedom to advertise sexual desires and preferences in the media and to perform sexual acts and exhibit private parts, even on television and the Internet.

Freedom to request the state and some churches to marry people of the same sex. "Why not?" they claim, as some priests and bishops are openly homosexual.

Freedom to live with someone of the same sex as "husband and wife."

Freedom to belong to private/exclusive clubs where members practise exchange of partners for sexual pleasure and prefer to go naked, even with their children in tow.

Weird freedoms such as freedom to pierce or tattoo any part of the body, including private parts.

Freedom of homosexuals to demonstrate publicly, publish their newspapers, openly criticize church and government actions that discriminate against or exclude homosexuals from certain activities. They even talk of having (and actually have) their own children through adoption and surrogate motherhood, despite the fact that they are homosexuals.

Other sexual freedoms according to people's whims and caprices.

This *sexual revolution* has resulted in, among other things:

A lot of adultery and divorce cases, producing delinquent children in their wakes.

Increased abortion rate (more than 700 daily in the USA alone)

Increased use of contraceptives by females, including teenagers (leading to destruction of the womb and inability to be pregnant)

Sterilization of some women (and some men) in various forms

Serious masturbation and the use of artificial sex objects to satisfy sexual desires.

Bolder moves by abortion proponents

More open practice of homosexuality, among other demeaning sexual acts, as if this behavior is natural and right.

Sometimes these days, the more you look at a person to help determine the sex, the more confused you become. What you see confuses you. In the process, you do not know how to exchange pleasantries or extend courtesies according to the sex of the person standing before, or sitting near, you.

Where does freedom really begin and end? Is anybody really free to do whatever they like at any time and place without any restrictions whatsoever? Even nature has its set of laws that must always be obeyed by all living and nonliving things. *There is therefore no such thing as absolute freedom; otherwise there will be chaos.* Freedom and responsibility should go together. Your freedom stops where someone else's right begins.

People should look around and see for themselves that even though man was born free, everywhere he is in one form of chain or another, to avoid chaos and to respect the age-old adage: "Live and let live."

There is so much to say about this that an entirely new book may need to be written.

Photographs and social reception

As has been mentioned previously, all the external ceremonies and lavish entertainment have nothing to do with the success or failure of a marriage. Everything that makes for success or failure is in the minds of the couple and their attitude to situations from this day forward. This is now the time for them to start saying and doing all things that will ensure the success of their marriage. They are now mature persons capable of bringing life into the world, fending for themselves and others around them. This is the time for them to stop listening to gossips from destructive, cowardly, and jealous friends and relations. With reasonable determination and prayers, all should be well.

50

After the formal ceremony is over, there is the social reception including taking of photographs, which can be billed "the mother of all photographs." A lot of time and postures go into this, with everyone who has ever been associated with the newlyweds wanting to be photographed with them exclusively. These include in-laws, special friends, classmates, coworkers, members of special meeting groups and even those who have worn the same kind of dress for the wedding. All sorts of groups claim special intimacy with the bride and groom on this day and so deserve to be treated specially. The bride and groom should understand and try to accommodate everyone as far as possible.

The master of ceremonies should be able to handle this; otherwise photographers could have a field day and be smiling all the way to the bank.

Some couples like a short reception while others prefer all day/night party. Couples should not, in any case, outstretch themselves. They may need all the energy to consummate their marriage at night, particularly if both of them have not had sex before this time. They should not expect that all arrangements would be 100 percent perfect. For instance, some guests may be well served while others go without. The person proposing the toast may forget to ask guests to rise up for the toast and clinking of glasses. Some gifts may be stolen. However, a good and agile chairman, an alert master of ceremonies, and other assistants will ensure that the social reception succeeds, with no major ugly incidents.

Going on honeymoon

If there is any intention to go on honeymoon on the same day, you should not forget to leave the reception venue early and pick up your traveling bags in time for the trip. Some honeymoons may be quite elaborate or expensive and may involve going abroad. This does not guarantee happiness in any way. Some couples have equally found happiness and marital bliss by checking into a first-class hotel in the same city. Still, others who are not financially buoyant have found happiness in going to relax in their simple homes. It is the couple's state of mind that matters in all of this, not their material wealth or extravagance.

As expected, a couple going on honeymoon usually has sex on their agenda, particularly the first timers. They will be alone most of the time, particularly at night. It is hoped they will enjoy sex sessions to the fullest, but sometimes, there can be disappointments for men if their wives do not cooperate fully at the beginning. Perhaps, such non-cooperative wives have read the advice of Ruth Smythers in her book <u>Instruction and Advice for the Young Bride</u>, which was published in 1894. It runs thus:

At this point.... let me concede one shocking truth. Some young women actually anticipate the wedding night ordeal with curiosity and pleasure! Beware such attitude! One cardinal rule of marriage should never be forgotten: give little, give seldom, and above all give grudgingly.

What a piece of advice! It will be interesting to find any sensible lady who will listen to this kind of advice in these days of sexual liberation and freedom when such women will be abandoned for others who are more liberally minded about sex. One truth, though, is that moderation is advised in all human actions. Too much or too little of anything may be bad.

Remembering wedding day

The bride and bridegroom should make the day a very happy one. It is usually said that there are *three important days* in the life of a person:

The day of birth
Wedding day, and
The day of death.

A couple is in a position to witness, enjoy and appreciate only one—their *wed-ding day.*

All the same, no matter how a man and a woman formalize their wedding, they are simply obeying Almighty God's injunction in the Holy Bible in Genesis 2:24

Therefore shall a man leave his father and his mother and shall cleave unto his wife, and they shall be one flesh.

This was later repeated by our Lord Jesus Christ in Matthew 19:5, the first of the four gospels.

Need more be said about the beauty of marriage? Are all those who are healthy, qualified, and financially viable listening? Do you know that time is ticking away against you, particularly if you are a lady, because of the biological clock?

Eligible bachelors and spinsters, where are you?

Highlights

Make up your mind early whether you want a formal wedding or not.
On the day of the wedding, watch the time and leave early for the venue.
Experienced people should handle social reception.
Feel relaxed and happy, despite mistakes here and there at the reception.
Some of these may be points for jokes later.
If you are going on honeymoon, plan for it and leave early.
Divorce or separation should not be in your dictionary.

Chapter 7
Living Together As Husband and Wife

"A loving and faithful wife is worth more than all the gold in the world."

Equality of partners

Marriage, like other aspects or milestones in life, should be taken seriously; otherwise partners should not have taken all the trouble to look for mates, date or court them, and go through rigorous and time-consuming ceremonies. Imagine the valuable time spent and all the risks to which partners were exposed while shuttling between their houses and other places! Each partner, as intended by nature, has shed their individualism for the greater benefit of the two, as a single unit. Both have now become one flesh, one family, and an indissoluble partnership in which both are equal. But the man, as intended by nature, becomes the <u>primus inter pares</u> (first among equals). This is because of his primary responsibility for protecting and providing for his family, even if he has to fight to the death. This responsibility has not changed for thousands, and perhaps millions, of years; only the form it takes has been changing from generation to generation. Thus, in ancient times when civil laws were nonexistent or undeveloped, when the law of the jungle reigned supreme, if a man's family member was attacked, he went straight ahead to defend him/her with any means at his disposal. This he did either through repelling the attacker or possibly killing him outright. It was the law of the survival of the fittest, some sort of "jungle justice."

These days, however, all the man in a similar position would need to do would be to call the police; otherwise, he might be charged with taking the law into his hands if he attacked the intruder.

While male chauvinism is not intended here, a look at the Holy Bible, Genesis 3:16, seems to imply that men should continue to dominate women in nearly all

53

departments of life except the bearing of children. God clearly stated this to *Eve* after she and Adam, the first couple (according to the Bible's Genesis), fell from grace to grass through disobeying God's orders by eating the forbidden fruit:

I will greatly multiply thy sorrow and thy conception; in sorrow thou shalt bring forth children and thy desire shall be to thy husband, and *he shall rule over thee.*

You are free to check this out from the Holy Bible and other religious books. The position, as mentioned above, has not changed since the creation of the world and may not change, despite the hue and cry from various female liberation movements throughout the world. Furthermore, women have not made the matter any better, as they do not even seem to trust themselves or their capabilities. You may recall that some women who had opportunity to rule as prime ministers or presidents or queens never appointed many women to their cabinets. In fact, their closest advisers were men and have remained men to this day. In the realm of politics and public life, men appear to have gained the upper hand for various reasons. There is no need to go into details here. Thus, human beings cannot undo what nature has done and should not try to; otherwise more problems may be created.

Division of responsibilities

It should be remembered that human beings are not quite different from the lower animals in many ways. If you watch the latter in their natural habitats, you will observe that a male usually gathers females (in a harem) and fights off other male intruders who try to lure away or mate with females in his territory. Animals, like humans, are quite territorial. Nations (such as Israel/Palestine, India/Pakistan, Britain/Argentina, etc) have gone to war over land, even in modern times. People and communities have also fought themselves over land matters. A male animal is therefore not different. This is one of the key functions in life for him: to defend his territory, to control the females, to defend them with all his might, even unto the death. If he loses a fight to a rival male, he loses his females and territory to the victorious male. Even in the wider world, nations have had to go to war over female matters. A good example from ancient literature is The Trojan War involving beautiful Helen of Troy (in <u>The Iliad</u> by Homer) in ancient Greek epic.

In the Middle Ages and a little before, a rich man with several wives was able to maintain his harem and enforce discipline within his household. Each one of them, wives and children, had their contributions to make toward the welfare of the entire family. If the man felt that his wives needed extra protection from other men, all he had to do was employ the services of slaves whom he castrated so that they would have nothing to do with his wives while they did their security job. In more recent times, as an alternative to castrated slaves, rich men having harems have had to employ "natural eunuchs" who had never experienced or maintained any erection. Everyone was reasonably happy, with proper division of labor under which all knew their responsibilities. There was hardly any bickering or complaint, even from castrated slaves, who received so many favors from their masters.

54

These days, it is easy for security guards, butlers, equestrians, photographers, and others to fall in love with members of the royal household they are supposed to protect or teach, and later spill the secrets to the tabloids for cash.

In today's world, however, particularly in advanced or so-called developed countries, such polygamous practices are outdated and will never work in these societies that have since accepted monogamy as a way of life. This has been forced down on men by Church doctrine, the Holy Bible (the New Testament in particular), economic hardship, and civil laws on equality of the sexes, in order to have more equitable, disciplined, and affluent societies. Through increasing urbanization, with education reaching more women than ever before and with other enlightenment programs and the pursuit of equal rights and opportunities for, and by, women all over the world, the old family ties and responsibilities are gradually dying out, even in the last strongholds.

Under such a system as was practised in the past, men were outgoing and almost single-handedly provided for their families, while women stayed at home and took care of domestic chores and children. This has to be understood by modern couples.

Accordingly, adjustments and compromises have to be made by a modern husband and his wife if they want their marriage to succeed. Marriage is like a lucky dip. Take whatever comes out of it and make the best use of it, with serious commitment. Like everybody who expects A in an examination, it is good to have high hopes and be optimistic. Sometimes, however, the score may be B or C and many are happy with this because the alternative, failure, is worse. The same thing applies to marriage—making do with the partner you have, no matter any imperfections, rather than having none.

It is now goodbye to fulltime housewives and welcome to professional women, working wives and mothers. The good old days for men are gone and may never come back. This does not mean that the modern man does not enjoy freedoms or privileges. Unfortunately, women, despite their increasingly successful emancipation, have to take care of children. They also perform a disproportionate amount of domestic chores. This is so principally because of their nature as women and the training they have received in taking care of the home front. A woman who does not do this may not find happiness as a wife and mother.

Thus, a modern couple should share family responsibilities in accordance with their abilities, convenience, and natural instincts without forcing the other party to part with funds or spend time on domestic chores. The man knows that as the head of his family he should pay rent or mortgage, pay school fees for children, pay car note, provide food money, and occasionally buy gifts for his wife if his income is sufficient. The role of the wife in all of this is to *lend support* to her husband in various ways including paying for some services such as electricity, telephone, gas, and water, etc. if she is working. In some homes, couples have found it convenient to pool all cash resources together in **a joint bank account** from which all bills are settled. Still, other couples have found it convenient to almost "legislate to the letter" what each partner is to bear while keeping their incomes *separate*. All of this requires discussion, understanding, and *some equity* in the sharing of the family burden. These days, too, some husbands may find themselves taking care of the home front while their wives go to work and become the breadwinners. However, women should be careful not to be bossy toward their better halves in order to avoid quarrels. Since who pays the piper dictates the tune, some women may take undue advantage, as providers for the family, to treat their husbands as domestic servants and do whatever they like. They should remember that no condition is permanent.

Times of adversity/hardship

Whatever method or system you decide on, you should remember that both of you are working for the common interest of the entire family. There may be times, although this is not to be prayed for, when a partner will be out of work. What then happens to expenses that are supposed to be borne by the unemployed partner? Here then lies the true test of love, which is very easy to say or promise but difficult to show in many trying situations in life. If you really love yourselves, the one who is employed should be able to continue meeting family expenses as far as possible. Consumption of food and usage of utilities should be reduced, and, where necessary, two meals per day rather than three could be taken, using a formula which people from "battered economies" of the world refer to as 0-1-1, 1-0-1, or 1-1-0. This formula is actually used for survival purposes. A ridiculous formula such as 1/2- 1/2- 1 or something similar is not unheard of. This means that half the normal ration is taken in the morning, the same reduced quantity is taken in the afternoon and one fairly full meal is then taken in the evening. Out there in the world, it is not impossible to have 0—0—0 formula in countries experiencing serious drought or famine. Even with all these formulae, many still eat like kings in the morning, like princes/dukes in the afternoon, and like paupers at night, if necessary. The family purse and problems will dictate the kind of meals to be taken and how many times a day.

If necessary, wasting assets such as cars (provided alternatives such as bus or train service are available) can be sold to make ends meet. Even one's residence can be changed to a cheaper one, through paying a lower rent or mortgage. Adjustment of a couple's lifestyle to fit the situation at hand becomes almost imperative. Where cash savings have been made, these will go a long way in meeting some expenses.

Thus living together entails *making so many sacrifices* by both partners and close relations in trying times. For many couples, all times seem to be "trying." But that is life and their cross to bear. Like our Lord Jesus Christ, they may be lucky to see a Simon of Cyrene or a Veronica help them lift the cross briefly and comfort them respectively. But the cross is theirs and theirs alone to carry. A man should therefore generally see it as his responsibility to provide the necessary wherewithal for his family while a woman should generally see it as her responsibility to blend this wherewithal in the best interest of the family. Women are very good at economizing and putting things together, particularly if they have been brought up in a rural or countryside setting.

Both partners should see that they *compliment each other* from time to time, especially if they have done something extraordinary or have worked very hard.

Doing things together

Living together also means *sharing things and resources.* Nothing belongs exclusively to one partner. One partner's troubles or setbacks are equally the other partner's troubles. One partner's success or triumph is equally the other partner's success. If one party is mourning, the other should join in, even if only symbolically, and share the sorrows. If one party is celebrating, the other should join in the celebrations. Living together invariably means *doing so many things together* or in common such as:

Eating
Sleeping (and what follows naturally)
Praying
Going out to events or on holidays
Visiting friends and relations
Sharing the day's events and jokes
Celebrating
Mourning, etc.
Playing with or teaching the children.
Watching television
Solving problems, etc.

Doing things together increases the love for one's partner and makes you both inseparable. A partner should take some interest in the office or academic work of the spouse and get to know their friends, relations, coworkers, classmates, and leisure activities that both of them can share. In all of this, there may be occasional disagreements or modifications to suit a partner. The other partner should yield if there is nothing seriously at stake. Partners should remember always that they are now responsible persons with a family and that their lifestyles should be consistent with their background, level of income, simplicity and humility and other circumstances of their situation, devoid of pride, arrogance, and lack of feelings for the plight of neighbors and relations. The more complex your lifestyle, the unhappier and less secure you feel. The opposite is almost true if you live a simple life, all things being equal.

Both partners, along with their children, should *take health matters seriously,* ensuring that they exercise regularly and take good foods such as fibers, fruits, protein, low fat milk, white meat, fish, vegetables etc. They should ensure, too, that they all go for medical checkup periodically.

Celebrating events

Furthermore, living together means that *certain events have to be remembered and celebrated,* as convenience and finance permit. There are events that are special to both partners such as their wedding anniversaries and birthdays. On such occasions, they may wish to celebrate with close friends and relations particularly for landmark birthdays and anniversaries such as fortieth, fiftieth, sixtieth, or seventieth birthday or tenth, twentieth, or fortieth wedding anniversary. On other occasions, they may choose to celebrate the events quietly after prayers including snuggling up to each other later in the quietness of their bedroom. If both of them are in the mood, they can try "other things" while they are still holding hands. Each partner should also surprise the spouse with *inexpensive but appropriate gifts and cards* on personal anniversaries. Dining out and even going on holiday together will also be fine if their pocket permits; otherwise they should stay at home with the kids and watch special films or movies. They should not forget to celebrate their children's birthday landmarks such as first, fifth, tenth, and eighteenth or twenty-first. Children should be taught humility and simplicity in all of this. There are always many events and occasions to celebrate. Flamboyance is not necessary. Above all, everybody should always be in the right frame of mind. In this way, everyone's happiness, even if they are celebrating in poverty, will be assured.

Equally important, they *should not forget to crack jokes and smile* from time to time. These do help to oil the love between partners and ease tension. Life is always full of tensions. Jokes help a lot to diffuse them. Couples prolong their lives through this process and by having satisfactory sexual relationship. Except you are the serious-minded type who has been brought up in the Spartan and monastic style of total silence and a stern-looking face, you should learn to appreciate jokes, smile regularly, see the funny side of life or actions and ease any tension building up. You can practically joke about anything from immediate surroundings, office or school to your own person. Every day, you see funny things and behaviors. You should joke about them while narrating them to your partner and others around you. For instance, on the personal side, if your partner is much taller or fatter than you are, you can joke about it in appropriate circumstances. The way someone eats, walks, sits, talks, dances, writes, or laughs can be good subjects for jokes. People should open their eyes and ears to see and hear a lot of jokes from local areas and around the world.

A woman's cornerstone position in a home

Living together happily has been recognized since God created human beings. Hear what St. Paul says in his Epistle to the Ephesians 5:22-24:

Wives, be subject to your husbands, as to the Lord. For the husband is the head of the wife, as Christ is the head of the Church and is himself its Savior. As the Church is subject to Christ, so let wives also be subject in everything to their husbands. Husbands, love your wives, as Christ loved the Church and gave himself up for her, that He might sanctify her, having cleansed her by the washing of water with the word that He might present the Church to Himself in splendor, without spot or wrinkle or any such thing, that she might be holy without blemish. Even so, *husbands should love their wives as their own bodies. He who loves his wife loves himself.* For no man ever hates his own flesh, but nourishes and cherishes it, as Christ does the Church, because we are members of His body. For this

reason, a man shall leave his father and mother and be joined to his wife, and the two shall become one flesh. This mystery is a profound one and I am saying that it refers to Christ and the Church; however, let each one of you love his wife as himself, and let the wife see that she respects her husband.

St. Paul says it all, even though he and some of the apostles and disciples were celibate.

St. Peter, on the other hand, was well married. He equally exhorts women to be submissive to their husbands, as seen in Chapter 3 of his First Epistle to the Galatians. The same theme runs through Chapter 3:7 as follows:

Likewise, you husbands live considerately with your wives, bestowing honor on the woman as the weaker sex, since you are joint heirs of the grace of life, in order that your prayers may not be hindered.

Both saints and founding fathers of the early Church, no doubt, had inspiration from God to say all these things.

Once a husband shows love toward his wife and children, and the wife respects him and his views (after presenting hers), a happy home is made. A man who has no happy home (as opposed to a house) to return to after each day's toil may not find any fulfillment in life. He will be lonely and depressed. Even if he decides to have extramarital affairs, he will never be satisfied or happy, thinking of health and other implications from time to time. If he is a celebrity or a highly placed or powerful figure, he should also think of the scandal, which the press will capitalize upon to sell their papers.

A woman, whether a man likes it or not, is the *cornerstone in a home.* All the children mill around her. Her husband has 100 percent confidence in her ability to take charge when he is away. The children look up to her for their welfare and her husband does likewise. She keeps the home running. Ironically, both husband and children are usually unable to look after the woman of the house when she is sick. The whole house then seems disorganized. The woman of the house has tremendous influence over the children much more than the man, since she feeds them and spends longer time with them. Children take complaints to their mothers first. Where necessary, they then present the problems to their fathers through their mothers who act as "liaison officers" or intermediaries. A woman usually oversees everything that happens at home and is ready to recount events in great detail. Apart from taking major decisions, providing some of the funds and helping with very difficult jobs around the home, a man usually has a casual attitude to what happens in his home. He is usually never available—"London today, New York tomorrow, always traveling or spending time at board meetings with visible and invisible friends," as one slogan aptly puts it.

If a woman is not happy, her home is certain to "collapse" sooner or later. Men should recognize what wives can do for them and learn to love and cherish them. There is no other way, if they want happy homes.

By the way, women influence men's lives a lot, from the cradle to the grave without men knowing it. A baby boy, child, or teenager is influenced by his mother. A middle-aged man is influenced by his wife. In his old age or twilight years, it is still the same wife or perhaps his daughters who help him to live out his old age.

Men, in their macho image, should therefore avoid humiliating women in any way, except the social deviants and those who want to involve men in wrongdoing to which they do not consent. Men should also not take advantage of women because of their presumed physical weakness. If women discover this, they may be ruthless. Who then can blame them?

Partners should watch their moods. There are times when the world around a partner seems to be collapsing due to bad news received or other problems on the ground. A state of melancholy is quite common. The other partner who is better at absorbing shocks or problems should help by pouring out encouraging or soothing words.

The worth of a loving wife in a home has been touched upon in so many places by the Holy Bible and other holy books and writings. Husbands should understand clearly that they might not be able to make it alone without their wives by their sides. Even though women tend to be most hurt emotionally when marriages fail, it is far easier for them to cope when they are alone than it is for men.

Assuming, in the unlikely event, that either men only or women only are to be chosen to exist in the universe, nature will find it easier to dispense or do away with men than women.

Apart from sperm women require for pregnancy, they need nothing else from men to keep the human race going. Women have wombs, fallopian tubes, ovaries, vaginas, and breasts for suckling the young, as well as appropriate hormones for the well being of the fetuses. Sperm can, of course, be stored and used as and when required by women.

For these and other reasons, women's bodies are regarded as sacred (and treated with respect) in virtually all parts of the world. In fact, medical research seems to suggest that during the primitive stages of pregnancy, all babies (male or female), by natural default, are formed like female until production of male hormones, e.g. testosterone. These then enable male organs to be formed from the female "template." Christians and other believers of the creation story may doubt this, as the Bible clearly states that Eve was created after Adam and, in fact, she was formed from Adam's rib.

Never mind the lives and actions of deviants such as prostitutes and so-called sex models (e.g., strippers, escort service girls, etc.) who tend to cheapen women. They are a necessary evil. This is nature at work again.

However, nature has good reasons for men and women to coexist and reproduce themselves, with appropriate division of labor between them. The emotions displayed by a couple during a sexual encounter and the use of a man's penis to actually deposit sperm into a woman's womb are all designed by nature for special purposes. These assist in producing healthy children, who will be loved by their parents unconditionally and who will equally love their parents when they grow up.

As previously mentioned, so many books and writings are available in which the virtues of a wife are elaborately praised. The Book of Proverbs in the Holy Bible states thus in **31:10-31**

> **Who can find a virtuous wife? For her worth is far above rubies (money). The heart of her husband safely trusts her; so he will have no lack of gain. She does him good and not evil all the days of her life. She seeks wool and flax and willingly works with her hands....She also rises while it is yet night and provides food for her household and a portion for her maid-servants....Her children rise up and call her blessed; her husband also, and he praises her....Charm is deceitful and beauty is passing, but a woman who fears the Lord, she shall be praised....**

How still true this is, if one cares to look around! If there is doubt, people should watch married women (and even some spinsters) how they worry about, and plan for, the welfare of their families. This is true whether or not women are office workers, business executives, or are engaged in any other activities. Nature must have ensured all this in the wonderful plan for the continued existence of humanity. There must be a hormone (or is it maternal instinct?) in women that makes them have this feeling for the welfare of their families. If you watch lower animals in the jungle, you will see the same nature at work. Observe how lionesses kill animals and provide food for their cubs and the males in the pride or group. Lions sleep away most of the time but protect the pride in times of danger. Males in the jungle busy themselves fighting for the right to mate exclusively with the females. Human beings, of course, do the same thing but a little differently. Have people ever watched how men keep themselves busy while preparing to date women and what actually happens during the dating process— how all sorts of lies and half-truths in various forms are told, just to impress their dates and how wealth and power in various forms are displayed?

Whoever has a good wife should therefore appreciate her and love her as well. If a man does not have a good or cooperative partner, let him see if he can first change his attitude toward her. He is bound to see new and positive changes in her sooner or later, as she now learns to trust him again.

Quarrels and harmonious settlements

Remember that any relationship is a continuous learning process, and this, perhaps, makes it more exciting. You have to study your partner like you study a textbook: what makes your partner happy, sad, ill, and moody; what your partner likes, such as food, reading magazines, or watching television or making calls. Whatever it is, capitalize on the good aspects and deemphasize those areas that put your relationship in the cold. Again, living successfully together requires partners, as much as possible, *to close their eyes to certain things or behaviors they see, to close their ears to certain news or information or gossips they hear and to keep their lips sealed by not responding to all annoying remarks by their partners.*

Then and only then will they have peace of mind and happiness. But if they choose to hear everything, see everything, and respond to all gossips, then they should be ready to welcome loneliness, high blood pressure, anger, and sadness, all of which shorten the lifespan.

In this connection, if a partner annoys the spouse in any way and the argument or exchange of angry words heats up, the latter should not try to return angry words, as they are difficult to recall once they have been voiced. One partner may be naturally hot-tempered; so the other one should try to understand and remain silent if necessary. "Silence," it is said, "is the best answer to a fool." Silence, too, is "golden." When tempers cool off, you may gradually recall the incident in style. This could take from a few hours to as long as three days. *You should not take any decisions when you are angry* because you are not at your best nor are you thinking rationally. If you do, you may find, to your eternal regret, that the decision was made "under influence," and it may be too late when you realize this. Avoiding or staying away briefly from your partner when tempers are high helps to ensure that peace returns early to your home. At this point, the obviously guilty partner comes apologizing. If you were equally guilty, that is if you started the argument or problem, you may find both of you apologizing to yourselves simultaneously. This is how it should be. Then, you may laugh at last.

Is this approach not better than having acrimonious relationship under which no one admits any fault and that leaves both of you seething in anger for a long time? Couples should try it. It works. It never fails.

Ways to a mate's heart

Finally, a wife should remember, as the saying goes, that, "The way to a husband's heart is through his stomach." To this I would like to add some other ways to a man's heart—respecting him and making yourself reasonably and readily available when he wants you, during the day or at night.

A husband should also understand that the way to a wife's heart is loving her with all his heart; helping, flattering, and praising her at appropriate moments; and keeping his affairs away from her, if he has any. If not, she may shut off her heart against him forever. A man should remember always that money cannot buy a loving wife.

If you are rich, in relative terms, you should not treat your partner as a slave. After all, being rich and having a successful marriage are not mutually exclusive. Yet, the opposite is what many rich people believe and practise, to their eternal unhappiness through payment of alimony and child support etc.

No room for a perfectionist

Lastly, a married couple should realize early that marriage, like life, is full of changes and uncertainties. Nothing remains static for long. All the same, all things humanly possible should be done to ameliorate adverse changes. These will be mainly through actions from the first day of marriage through increasing positive actions leading to a secure and happy marriage, while decreasing or eliminating negative actions that tend to lead to problems, unhappiness or uncertainties. *Nobody should try to be a perfectionist at home or in the office.* With partners now living together (perhaps, with children) their lives can never be the same again.

The kitchen, bathroom, parlor, and bedrooms can never be as perfect as they used to be before marriage. When a partner or child falls short of expectations, you should temper your criticisms with appreciation. Positive criticisms rather than negative ones make more impact. As can be appreciated, there is a great deal of difference between the following sentences, both of which convey the same idea. However, one sentence has been cast differently for better reception by the person addressed:

<u>Group A</u>
1. "Do not make noise. I am reading."
2. "Darling, could you talk in a lower tone to enable me concentrate? Thank you."

<u>Group B</u>
1. "This dress you are wearing is so much out of date that you should throw it away or have it changed."
2. "My dear, why don't you wear that blue gown that emphasizes your curves and beauty instead of this one?"

As you can see, the person being addressed will respond negatively to the first sentence in each of the above groups, but is more likely to do what is required if the approach in the second sentence in each group is used. The same technique can be successfully applied to get children do the right things, applying the carrot or stick as circumstances dictate.

Highlights
Respect and love each other.
Learn to make sacrifices, compromises and adjustments at all times.
Accept whatever problem comes your way, with equanimity.
Joy, laughter, and jokes should feature in your relationship.
Do everything together as much as possible.
Celebrate when you must do so but also share any grief that comes along.
Do not try to be a perfectionist at home or in the office.
Softly spoken and appropriate words have more influence on a partner than commands or harshly spoken words.

Chapter 8
Dealing with Outsiders

"No one is, or should be, an isolated island."

Relations, friends, and in-laws

As everybody is well aware, nobody is an island to himself or herself. You cannot live alone and expect to be happy. Human beings are highly sociable animals, except, of course, nature has prepared you to be otherwise. Human beings from eternity have always lived in communities of varying sizes, have usually helped one another, done things together, and protected themselves and their properties under prevailing jungle laws or social contracts.

Thus, celebrating or dancing alone does not seem to make any sense except, perhaps, to a person of unsound mind. The more the number of participants or celebrants, the merrier the occasion should be. Remember the saying or slogan: "The more we are together, the happier, the merrier. The more we are together, the happier we shall be."

Even lower animals live together, hunt together, and protect themselves from intruding enemies, thus ensuring their continued existence, along with that of their descendants as envisaged by nature. **So, a couple should be ready to deal with people other than themselves and their children.** They include, but are not limited to, the following:

In-laws
Brothers and sisters
Aunts and uncles
Cousins
Nieces and nephews

Stepmothers and stepfathers
Mothers and fathers
Friends
Neighbors
Classmates and schoolmates
Office colleagues
Church and club members
Customers
Service providers
Public officers

A couple should be ready to share their joys and sorrows at all times. Even animals such as dogs, cows, horses, cats, goats, birds, and other pets should not be ignored because they are around you at all times.

It is quite easy to deal with these groups and keep in touch with as many as possible within each group. Do not shy away from identifying yourself with the group to which you appropriately belong. Participate actively in promoting the general well being of all groups you belong to. Note, too, that there are some groups to which you automatically belong, whether you like it or not. For instance, if there is an association for the ex-students of ABC College and you went through ABC College, you automatically belong to that association. You become an alumnus. However, remember that you cannot properly belong to the association or receive any benefits except you register as a member and keep its by-laws.

Your in-laws, who consented to your marriage, are probably the most difficult group to deal with. All the same, you must deal with them or identify yourself with them. A wise wife must remain friendly at all times with her in-laws and her husband's friends. When she has any problems with her husband, most probably bordering on infidelity, cruelty, or an irresponsible lifestyle, these people are the best and the first to approach to talk to her husband. It is they who will give her necessary support to deal with her husband's waywardness.

In some countries, in-laws constitute a powerful group and interfere with marriages a lot, creating serious problems for couples. Certain obligations are seen to be morally mandatory on a husband, e.g., burial expense of a father-in-law or a mother-in-law. In other situations or customary practices, a son-in-law is expected to help train members of the wife's family such as her brothers and sisters. From time to time, too, a son-in-law is expected to send "drinks" or gifts to his father in-law, to thank him for giving him a wife and to promote better son-in-law/father-in-law relationship. Some couples are lucky not to have moral responsibilities such as these.

There were reasons behind these arrangements, which worked reasonably well in the past but which have since begun to be ignored or fade away. This was a part of the "extended family system" or responsibility in many third world countries. There is nothing wrong with helping others, more so if the person who has been requested to do so had benefited from the system in the past. It is a way of being one's brother's keeper. Even developed nations have always been a part of this fellowship through responding with food, clothes, medicine, peace keeping troops, professional workers, and other resources during emergencies and tragedies within their territories and beyond. The system of state welfare services (extending help to those out of work and those who are disabled or sick) is similar to the extended family responsibility system practised in developing countries of Africa, Asia, and Latin America. In the first situation, it is the states that are *primarily* responsible, whereas in the second situation, it is the individuals that are *morally* responsible (of course, without any legal consequences).

If your in-laws need cash or help, you should be ready to assist up to what you can reasonably afford. They need not live with you. When you are pressured against your will, you can always put your foot down.

Some in-laws under your roof tend to build obstacles between you and your partner because they will never see things your own way or in the right perspective. They usually gossip about your lifestyle. Worse, some young relations have been known to develop amorous relationships with in-laws, to the eventual detriment of couples and their marriages. For these and other reasons, couples should be wary of admitting young in-laws into their homes for long periods.

Also to be watched are your blood relations, who are in the same group as in-laws. They may not see eye-to-eye with you in the way you live with your spouse. If they require help, give it if you can, but inform your partner lest you be accused of secretly helping only your relations.

As for the wife, her mother-in-law is the most important outsider she has to deal with. She has to learn to deal with her, respecting her views when it is necessary to do so, but also politely and tactically declining to do those things her mother-in-law suggests if she does not like them. She should not pick up any quarrel with her, but should always report to her husband whenever she has a clash with her. It is only her husband who can deal with his mother effectively and no body may ever hear of it. Then and only then will in-laws not call the wife any ugly names. As far as a mother-in-law is concerned, a wife can never do anything right for her son. Generally, mothers-in-law are by nature very nosy and like to know every detail about what goes on inside their sons' homes, including their bedrooms. If a wife is lucky, she could have a very good and cooperative mother in-law. She may be the wife's best friend and may even suggest ways to please her son and tell her all the tricks not in the books, to enable her secure her husband's attention at all times.

Fathers-in-law are generally never troublesome, so long as their daughters-in-law respect them and treat them to good food at all times.

So, if you are a wife, it is in your own interest to remain friendly with your in-laws and keep your marriage, or make them "enemies" and risk ruining your marriage, particularly if your husband is "mama's boy." If you are broad-minded and tactful, you should learn how to deal with the "devils" and the "angels" you find among your in-laws. Give both groups their dues, like giving to Caesar what is Caesar's and to God what is God's.

Moral/sexual laxity among in-laws and known examples

Still talking about in-laws, you should be very careful, and avoid any temptations to have sexual liaison with them. Many more husbands seem to be far more involved in these despicable or shameful acts than wives. This *insider involvement* could destroy one's marriage much more easily than sexual liaison with outsiders. Men have been known to fall in love with their mothers-in-law. Unfortunately, when men and women who are supposed to observe the no-go areas or liaisons are placed together in certain circumstances, close liaisons may be possible after a while, with one thing leading to another. Physically, there may be no difference between one man and another or between one woman and another. It is the mind, attitude, culture, law and training that make it possible to "differentiate" between one man and another or between one woman and another. When dangerous and forbidden liaisons take place, all hell is let loose and parties involved usually end up badly. In some societies, the parties may be ostracized for life while in others they may be killed or they themselves commit suicide because of the shame and ignominy involved, which they cannot bear to live with.

A few cases will illustrate the above points:

Case # 1

A successful businessman lived in the same house with his wife and mother-in-law. Over time, the man and his mother-in-law found themselves attracted to each other, as both had common interest in music, politics, and literature etc. His wife had other interests. The husband and wife, for various reasons, eventually separated. The man and his mother in-law, however, continued to stay in the same house, but were caught red-handed having sex by the ex-wife who had come visiting. After several overtures from friends and relations, the liaison ended, but it was too late for the ex-wife who had to undergo long psychiatric treatment to overcome the shock. You can imagine what would have happened to the ex-wife's disposition if she had been living under the same roof with them at the time of the incident. Both the man and his randy mother-in-law lost their minds in agreeing to the illicit liaison. One of them would have acted as a check on the excess of the other, with the advice or warning that sexual bounds were being exceeded. Yet, both chose to ignore the consequences of their illicit liaison. As a result, all of them lost out, as well as society.

Case # 2

A young husband with his wife moved to his mother-in-law's house, not yet able to afford his own home. With time, the man and his young and dashing mother-in-law developed illicit sexual liaison that eventually led to two divorces when they were caught red-handed by the father in-law of the man and husband of the randy mother-in-law. In other words, the father saw his own wife having sex with his son-in-law. What an abomination! What sexual indiscretion among adults could possibly be greater than this?

The young wife divorced her husband while the father-in-law divorced his randy and adulterous wife (the youngman's mother-in-law). But the story did not end there. As if to give their illicit relationship a stamp of approval, the shameless young husband and his amorous mother-in-law eloped to another location and continued the sexual liaison. Again, the young wife needed and obtained medical and psychiatric treatment to overcome this betrayal by her erstwhile "darling" husband and her "sweet" mother. Who else in the world could she have trusted more than her mother and her husband? Yet, these two failed her at the same time by engaging in unspeakable sexual liaison.

Case # 3

This last case is quite similar to the first two, but the end result is different. This was mainly due to the mature handling of the matter by the wife who was cheated or betrayed. In this our ever-changing world, economic necessity or convenience dictates people's actions sometimes, even where morals are at stake. Whoever wears the shoe knows where it pinches.

In this case, a married young man had been secretly admiring his beautiful mother-in-law, who was living with him and his wife. He disclosed his feelings to his mother-in-law who stupidly agreed to have dangerous sexual liaison with him. When the young wife became aware of the sexual liaison, she was heartbroken but did not want her marriage to end. Her heart was made of steel because she quietly but discontentedly accepted the liaison. She did not want to lose her husband or mother, hoping and praying that the shameful liaison would end soon. After all, her mother was always around to take care of her little children and perform domestic chores. How could she cope without her mother? This bothered her a lot while the love triangle lasted a few years, under the same roof.

Then the dangerous and shameless mama moved out when she found another lover and sanity was restored. What a wise decision by the wife! But the cost to her health and mental stability during this period is incalculable. What is not known is whether the man had sexual relations with his wife at the same time that the illicit liaison went on.

This kind of tolerant and forgiving wife deserves a prize and some recognition from all lovers of indissolubility of marriage and other social groups. She was a rare breed. She demonstrated tolerance, understanding, and patience in the entire process. She carried the wounds in her heart for many years and still managed to keep her marriage. Many marriages that failed would have been saved if the world had many of her type.

Dangerous or forbidden liaisons can destroy families and should be avoided at all costs. Once people are in love, particularly with regard to illicit liaisons, they become bolder before everyone. They gradually expose themselves, as they can no longer hide their feelings or actions. They throw caution to the wind and are eventually caught in disgrace.

In each of the above-mentioned cases, if those involved wanted extramarital relationship (assuming sexual inadequacy of their partners), they would have found willing partners outside, rather than succumbing to time-honored forbidden liaisons. Their marriages would have been intact and they would have been happier. Instead, they chose the road of destruction, to their eternal regret.

The partners in the above three cases committed relationship faux pas for the following reasons:

1. The partners were among the no-go or forbidden sexual liaisons
2. They chose the wrong place for sex
3. They chose the wrong time.

What could be worse for a man or a woman than combining all of the above?

In many ways, what concerns your in-laws and relations also concerns you. Visiting your in-laws and relations periodically with your partner or phoning them is good and should be practised, as they are a part of your life. Writing them once in a while is also welcome, as this helps to cement the bonds of relationship. If you are close to them, they will readily come to your assistance whenever you need them. Sending them valuable gifts, cards, and flowers is welcome. But be sure to send what will be appreciated, e.g., cards and flowers to those who are used to Western values. However, clothes, food, alcoholic liquor, jewelry and even money will be highly appreciated by those who are used to African, Latin American, and Asian values.

Friendly gossips

One word of advice is enough: beware of so-called friends!

Of course, the friends you made when you were single should not be ignored or thrown out. Obviously, because of your current attachment to your partner, you may not be able to spend as much time with them as before. You should call and visit them occasionally. You should also welcome their phone calls and visits. It is not always easy to detach yourself from old friends who may still share old values with you. New friends may come your way, but whether old or new, if your friends' lifestyles do not agree with yours and you cannot accommodate them, it is better to sever the relationship nicely rather than destroy your future.

Friends have been known to destroy happy marriages out of sheer jealousy. Women are particularly guilty of all sorts of gossips. They sometimes mislead friends into believing that their husbands treat them better or that life outside marriage is better. You are advised to stay away from such friends. They will destroy you if you listen to them. Some may even tell you that they cannot tolerate certain behaviors from their husbands, in order to set you up against your husband. You will then discover later that such gossipers tolerate worse behaviors from their own husbands.

To add to this, you must never discuss details of what happens inside your matrimonial home with any one. If someone is nosy about this information, it is obvious the person has ulterior motives. Furthermore, you should not run your partner down before friends or relations because when you are not with them, they laugh at you.

In this connection, the story is told about one well known "lady activist" (feminist) who went to a symposium to say all sorts of things about the way husbands "enslaved" wives. In the course of her lecture, she exhorted women never to give in but to challenge such men and request assistance from them in the performance of domestic chores, particularly with respect to working or professional women. She was praised and well hailed at the end of the lively lecture for being so bold and independent-minded.

Subsequently, one of the female admirers decided to visit this feminist at home to seek advice on some marital problems or concerns. She was shocked to see this "lady activist" doing virtually all the usual, traditional domestic chores—cleaning, cooking and washing clothes—while her husband relaxed, reading papers, and waiting for his supper. The visitor promptly left, excusing herself that she needed to go to the market before it was too late. Thereafter, she quickly resigned from the "feminist" organization and went back to continue performing her role as a good housewife, never quarrelling with her husband again over performance of domestic chores. Instead, she later persuaded her husband to employ a housemaid to assist her.

This is a classic example of one woman misleading other women by saying one thing in public and doing something different in private—sheer hypocrisy! Even if she practised what she preached and succeeded in her own home, there is no assurance that it will succeed elsewhere, as circumstances are different. Each marriage is unique and each couple should work out ways to ensure a lasting and happy relationship.

Sometimes, too, your friends could come around to tell you how they had seen your husband with another woman in his car or hotel, etc. Do not listen to them if you trust your husband. Even if you do not trust him, why should such friends come to tell you what will obviously hurt you and your marriage? If these friends love you, they should call your husband's attention to what he is doing and advise him to desist from such despicable behaviors in future, without involving you.

Generally, what you do not know, see or hear will definitely not hurt you. You do not even need to probe any further, lest you open Pandora's Box, to your eternal regret. Sometimes, you may see something and pretend to be blind. You may hear something and pretend to be deaf. You may also be told something hurtful and pretend to be dumb. All this is an effort on your part to keep the peace and not rock the boat—a big virtue that only a few men and women have.

Your neighbors

Neighbors should be treated like your friends, picking out those you wish to associate with, without staying aloof from others. Thus, *you should remain friendly without being friends.* This sounds rather paradoxical, but it can be practised. Neighbors can be particularly helpful in emergencies such as calling police, fire dept. or ambulance unit, or even looking after children in the absence of their parents.

Never borrow things continually, if at all, from them except you are very close and there is reciprocal borrowing, in order to avoid gossips and keep your honor or dignity. Treat their children as yours, but do not give them anything to eat or drink without their parents' consent. They may be allergic to some foods or drinks or may be required to abstain from them due to health problems.

Thus in dealing with these various groups, you should know your limits. Be close but not close enough, to avoid being known inside out. After all, you may have some secrets, which should remain so until the last day. In this way, those with bad motives will not be able to take undue advantage. Know when to call it quits with them. Your honor will then remain intact.

Highlights

Learn to deal with everybody who has connection with you through marriage and other associations.

Give everyone his or her due.

Learn to be friendly with all, but pick your friends.

Do not listen to gossips or act on them.

You need neighbors and friends, but know your limits.

Chapter 9

A Couple's Sex Life

"The beauty of sex or lovemaking is better appreciated when you have it with a loved one, at the right time and place, and you are in the right mood."

General sex life

Research has shown that virtually all animals, human beings included, have two major pre-occupations or instincts—survival and sex. Even though the survival instinct appears to be stronger than the sex instinct, there can be no survival without sex when the chips are down. The two instincts are related and interdependent. Animals must do all in their power to ensure their survival and that of their offspring by eating and defending themselves, even if this means killing an enemy. Over hundreds of thousands of years, animals have evolved several survival strategies: how to defend themselves against known and unknown enemies and what to eat and what not to eat, in order to prolong their lives. This has continued up to the present time in various forms. As soon as they are relaxed, they think of sex and take advantage of any available situation to satisfy their sexual urge. They also think of ways to make sex more interesting and enjoyable, including going to exotic places and using various paraphernalia now in the market. Through this process, continued existence of animals is reasonably assured and controlled, as designed by nature.

Therefore, there is no compelling reason why healthy and happy partners should not enjoy their sex lives to the fullest, without any inhibitions whatsoever. Having sex (or lovemaking, as some euphemists choose to distinguish) with a loved one is probably the climax of all love for your partner and it is a very beautiful experience.

By the way, there is apparently <u>no special school where sex is taught</u> and parents do not find it comfortable to discuss explosive sex matters with their children.

Parents usually go into details with their children about education, career, safety, friends, and general subject matters, but never about sex or sexual intercourse, let alone how to satisfy partners in the bedroom. No one seems to know why this is so. It might have something to do with our origins from the story of the creation when Adam and Eve found themselves naked and felt ashamed after eating the forbidden fruit.

As children mature into adults, they pick up information about sex (in words and pictures) from books, magazines, friends, classmates, and, these days, from television and the Internet. Their sex instinct comes into play as well, even from very early ages while still in the kindergarten. These days, too, there are many publications and videos from which a lot of visual knowledge is obtained about sex and relationships. Sex-related subjects, it seems, are usually better discussed with friends than with very close relations, particularly among children and young people.

Many men do not seem to mind if they have sex with females other than loved ones, so long as they satisfy their sexual urge. Unlike men, however, a majority of women (if not all) mind who their sex partners are and bring all emotions to bear on lovemaking. This is probably why women, unlike men, never forget the partners they have had sex with and the exact circumstances. Generally, men tend to satisfy their sexual urge with any women they can find, so long as they are apparently neat and fairly beautiful (with sex appeal) and won't put them in trouble. Men need not fall in love with their sex partners in order to enjoy sex. Women, on the other hand, generally tend to make love only with the men they love and can trust to keep the affair reasonably quiet. *Thus, loving and trusting a sex partner is of paramount importance to a woman.*

Sexual inhibitions/self-service

Lovemaking is so wonderful that it is difficult to explain it to someone who has not experienced it. So full of emotions, it cannot be enjoyed if you are in a **bad mood or are sick.** For a man, it is even worse as he may never have an erection, let alone penetrate, particularly if he has fever or is taking sedatives, tranquilizers or other medications that tend to weaken the sex urge. For a woman, her nipples will hardly stand erect and she will experience some dryness in her vagina, thus making it very difficult for her partner to penetrate fully without any pains. Some women suffer from *inadequate vaginal stimulation,* caused by inadequate production/release of relevant hormones. Thus, the labia and clitoris do not swell to the natural level. This is, perhaps, the female equivalent of male erectile dysfunction. Even if her partner succeeds in penetrating, she is bound to jettison him as soon as she starts feeling some pains because of her dryness There are ways to handle this kind of problem, at least through appropriate lubrication with oil or jelly before sex, or, more importantly, through a fairly prolonged foreplay, so that both partners enjoy their lovemaking. But a male partner has to be careful here, lest he discharge before the actual sexual encounter begins. It goes without saying that men and women with any form of sexual inadequacy should work with their doctors to find solutions to their problems. New treatments for some of these problems are being discovered on a regular basis.

Another inhibiting factor is fear, particularly on the part of the man. If a man shows signs of fear, for whatever reason, perhaps for what he has done wrongly or if he has been scared by an enemy through threats to his life or those of loved ones, it is usually difficult for him to have an erection in a short time, if at all. In the same way, if he **feels insecure** because he has no job or money, this affects his mood adversely. These are but a few examples of inhibiting factors. Others include the level of hygiene maintained by the couple, especially the woman and her level of readiness or cooperation with her intended sex partner.

A couple should understand these and not dismiss them offhand if they are to enjoy their sex life. Virtually everyone who is human must contend with one problem or another from time to time. The matter should be well handled by a couple who should not start accusing themselves of lack of interest in the other partner or unfaithfulness, as some women are fond of doing.

Thus a partner who is not in the right mood for sex can save the situation by quickly telling his or her partner and excusing himself/herself with apologies. A woman who is having her menstrual flow should tell her husband well in advance so that he does not plan to have sex, then have a sleepless night and be disappointed in the end. With this advance information, he should be able to sleep peacefully. In this connection, women seem to believe that their partners should study their menstrual cycle and thus know when sex will not be available. Men, unfortunately, are not good timekeepers in this respect, as they want their partners to be available for sex at all times.

In the same way, a woman should not unnecessarily refuse a man's sexual advances, as the man may not sleep until he has had his way, with her cooperation. Unnecessary delay or refusal could be an inhibiting factor for the man who, despite his earlier heightened arousal, may find it difficult to maintain an erection for long.

All the same, even if a partner is sick or is not in the right mood for sex, the two of them can still hold hands, kiss, or snuggle up to each other. After all, marriage is not all lovemaking. A man should therefore try to show some understanding if his wife refuses him sex. But invariably, he does not. He feels it is his right to have it at any time and place without taking his wife's feelings into consideration. Men seem to forget that women usually pick up the pieces after sex—possible pregnancy, bleeding, pains, and emotional disturbance, not to mention the possibility of contracting diseases from philandering husbands. For these reasons, she should be allowed to take the decision after weighing all risks. Men, on the other hand, just walk away after a sex bout, with little or no risks. Sometimes, however, wives with a lot of understanding and experience in this field reluctantly meet their husbands' requests half-way, that is, by participating reluctantly only up to 50 percent of normal performance. They do this by lying still or almost motionless in one position like a log of wood, while their fully charged husbands struggle endlessly to satisfy themselves and relieve themselves of the "load" they are carrying. This is what an experienced friend appropriately referred to as "self-service," in apparent reference to the way people serve themselves in restaurants or supermarkets when they go out to buy things, with little or no assistance from staff standing by.

This self-service approach is sometimes necessary and used when children wake up in the night and demand the attention of their mothers. Invariably, this is the time couples want to have sex. How children know this and want to disrupt their parents' pleasure is really mysterious. If necessary, mothers could soothe the children with one or both hands while they assist their already aroused husbands to have some satisfaction and go back to sleep.

In this kind of situation, both the men and their wives are left without full satisfaction, but at least they have met themselves halfway.

Women should also understand that if they constantly use sex as a weapon against their husbands, the latter may fall into the hands of loose and more cooperative ladies, to the detriment of such sex-as-a-weapon wives. After all, an actual sex session including foreplay, excluding those using drugs to enhance their staying power for entertainment purposes, rarely lasts beyond fifteen minutes.

Another aspect of sexual relationship with a loved one relates to the use of coitus interruptus (or interruption of sexual intercourse) by a partner to punish a spouse. Sexual relationship is supposed to be *consensual*. In these days of constant rape accusations against men, only women can say if their consent had been given and not withdrawn before commencement of, or during, a sexual liaison. Once it begins, it is expected that it should be completed and not unduly interrupted for a flimsy excuse. Cases abound in which spouses have been found guilty for unduly interrupting sex and have been successfully used as a basis for divorce. Understandably, a woman is entitled to withdraw her consent for various reasons ranging from fear of pregnancy or picking up a disease to a feeling of unusual pain. Perhaps she is no longer in the mood for sex. This is quite mercurial, but it is a part of women's nature.

However, men should be very careful when having sexual liaisons with ladies who are not their wives, as the former can claim that they withdrew their consent after the sexual act had begun and that their partners raped them by failing to withdraw immediately after their consent was withdrawn. This, as can be seen, is a dangerous game. It is extremely difficult to know who is telling the truth in each circumstance. So the general advice is: Beware! Know the kind of things your intended partner is capable of doing before you ruin your life in a sexual encounter that may last only a few flying minutes.

Unfortunately, many prominent men have been caught in this trap. The price? Jail terms, fines, loss of business or contract, and public humiliation, inter alia.

Sex balancing acts in nature

Another aspect of men's lives that women should understand is that men, by nature, are far more sexually active than women. The external position of men's active sex organs makes them "feel randy" and have the urge or feelings for sex as quickly as possible. Merely looking at a beautiful, slightly clad, or naked woman in person or in pictures is enough to arouse them, even if slightly. At least people have heard of or seen "peeping Toms" but not "peeping Joans or Catherines." In addition, men's sex hormones, which are embedded in their bodies, ensure that their sex lives are very active, pushing them, so to say, to make the first move and ask attractive women for dates from which other things may follow. Nature has designed it this way to ensure perpetuation of the human race. At the same time, the same nature, trying to create a balance, ensures that men do not have their way at all times, so that Mother Earth is not overpopulated. All these, among others, are natural means of checking population explosion.

Thus:

Men's erection fails them sometimes, if not frequently; in which case no penetration is possible even with the greatest effort.

Women have their menstrual periods, during which time sex is not enjoyed or had. In some cultures, it is taboo to have sex at this time.

Women generally refuse to have sex when they are ovulating, except they want to be pregnant, and then take the chance. They tell their partners that this is a bad or dangerous time to have sex.

Some men are impotent and are incapable of having any erection. Some have one form of erectile dysfunction or another. The exact cause should be found to see if it is treatable.

Women suckle their newborn babies for four to six months or even one year, during which period there may be no sex or pregnancy in general.

Women refuse men's advances frequently.

Some women are infertile and so cannot be pregnant through natural processes. These days, it is possible to fertilize an egg in a test tube in a laboratory environment and implant it in the womb (IVF), giving rise to what people generally refer to as "a test-tube baby." This method has its limitations, is expensive beyond the reach of low-wage earners and carries more risks for the baby than those conceived through old-fashioned methods.

A sperm's life is very short and may end before reaching a woman's egg for fertilization to take place.

Only *one sperm* out of *so many millions* ejaculated by a man during sex can fertilize an egg. Others die off or gradually whither away. The reason is not farfetched. Imagine being in an important race with several people to break the tape first, after a long and tortuous journey or competition!

Some men have very low sperm count, making it difficult for them to impregnate women. Thus, men also suffer decreased fertility for various reasons ranging from twisted testicles and defects in ejaculatory duct/pituitary gland, hormonal deficiency, to other factors such as smoking, drug usage, and alcoholism.

Women must agree or say "yes" before sex can take place (except in rape cases). Men make an offer or suggestion to have sex. It is up to women to accept. A good percentage will usually refuse because it is at the wrong time or place, or they are not in the mood or do not have the right partners.

Some women have twisted fallopian tubes, underdeveloped wombs, and other disabilities in the reproductive system, making pregnancy impossible or at least difficult. Other problems include fibrosis in the womb, ovarian cyst, ovulation problems, and many other defects which prevent or delay pregnancy until they are treated to correct the problems.

Pregnancies last, on the average, eight to nine months, lengthening the time another conception may take place. Animals with very high mortality rates (rats for instance) usually have very short pregnancy periods and produce many babies at the same time. Here again nature is trying to help animals preserve their species when the odds of survival are so much against them.

Women experience menopause, on the average, between their fortieth and fiftieth year. When this built-in biological clock sets in, there can be no more pregnancies, at least through natural processes. Instead, they experience hot flashes, probably as a result of loss of some female hormones at menopause such as estrogen.

The hormone, testosterone, is inadequate in some men, making them have a cool attitude toward sex, i.e., not much desire for sex.

It is important to remember that sexual dysfunction does not relate only to men's impotence. The two sexes usually experience failures as they grow older. The failure may be due to one or more of so many factors: poor blood circulation, diabetes, heart problem, high blood pressure, stress, alcoholism, and medications that go with these medical problems. For the lady, intercourse may not be pleasurable. In fact it may be painful due to dryness and a thinning of the vaginal wall.

The inadequacy with respect to testosterone can be corrected through appropriate medication, eating certain foods, and by exercises.

These and other controls have been put in place by Mother Nature. All men and women should therefore be aware of these and try to accommodate them if associated problems cannot be solved.

On the other hand, women's sex organs are embedded in their bodies. For this reason, women are difficult or slow to arouse. Even when they see naked men in person or in pictures, they tend to show disgust or disapproval, unlike men in the case of naked women. Of course, their sex hormones generally are less active than men's. All of this, coupled with the early training they received (to avoid teenage and unwanted pregnancies by rebuffing men's sexual advances, to close their legs properly when seated, and to avoid exposing their bodies through under-dressing) makes them less receptive, at least initially, to men's requests for sexual favors. This initial rebuff makes them less cheap and earns them some respect before men. Of course, prostitutes, sex models (the "modern" name for those in this time-honored profession), and others under various guises who want to make a living through commercial sex and exhibition of naked bodies are exceptions. As is well known, every general rule has an exception.

Men should understand early that it is women who control men's sex lives. A man makes advances, but it is up to the woman to say "yes" or "no." It is when she says "yes" that the deal is confirmed and sealed. ***So, it is the woman who eventu - ally chooses her sex partner, the time and place to have sex and the manner or style of sex she wants, not the man.*** This seems right as she and she alone will bear the burden of any resulting pregnancy or shame associated with all of this, while the man, in his usual characteristic manner, wanders off, perhaps into the waiting arms of another woman.

It is also more or less the rule in the lower animal kingdom. Males display their feathers, horns, manes, and other male characteristics to their female counterparts. These males follow their female counterparts for a long time and court them in various ways before the females yield to the males' sexual advances. Thereafter, the males wander off - typical of their human, male relatives.

You should watch domestic animals such as dogs, horses, cats, goats, sheep, cows, or chicken if you are unable to watch wild animals. Females do not yield easily to the sexual advances from males except they have been courted. There are exceptions to these observations, however, just as there are exceptions to almost every rule. Thus, in certain species, it is the females that go looking for the males.

Some men are less active than others in sex matters. These should marry sexually active women if the former are to enjoy sex. Thus, some women are more sexually active than others, are "sex-pots" and are in a position to initiate sexual liaisons. These sex-pots remain sexually aroused long after their male partners have run out of "steam" and crave for more action from their reluctant and tired partners. These, as mentioned above, should marry sexually inactive males for balance.

Watch the lower animals in their natural habitats. You will see all of the above observations in human beings manifesting themselves. Animals do not usually mate outside their heat periods and even at that, females do reject male advances until they are ready to accept them. Females look for the best among the males to ensure healthy offspring. Males cannot force their way, as the females "cover" their external sex organs very well with their tails and dribble the males for some time before finally accepting them, if at all. Females tend to keep permanent male partners for long but will not be jealous if males stray a little bit. Males also compete for females in the lower animal kingdoms by fighting rivals fiercely and are ready to fight to the death should other males enter their marked-out territories.

How true this is in the higher animal kingdom of human beings! Men have fought and even killed themselves because of women. Women have also fought and even killed fellow women because of men. In some primitive societies, endurance tests such as horsewhipping or wrestling were given (and are still given) to bachelors in order to be certain of their ability to keep, protect and satisfy women they intended (or intend) to marry. These days, such endurance tests may include having a college degree or professional certification or training for a job, a good job, and a house or an apartment for a suitor.

Being in the mood/sexual positions

If a man therefore plans to have sex with his partner, he should try to put her in the proper mood, well in advance of the actual time planned for sex. Softly spoken words or praises along with flattery, and a few drinks while discussing or watching television can help to put her in the right mood for sex. Sometimes, this role is reversed and it is the woman who now tries to seduce her man by putting on good makeup, flashy or see-through nightgown and talking to her husband nicely, all this after a very good meal. The husband, from experience, knows what next to do. Nobody will teach him his "job"!

Of course, where there are children, a couple should wait until they have all gone to bed. If other adults are present, then the randy couple should simply excuse themselves and go into their usual bedroom or any other appropriate place.

Inside the room, the couple should have no inhibitions whatsoever, as both are adults, are married, and are supposed to enjoy their sex life. The wife, in particular, should not bring into the bedroom problems or arguments she had during the day or in the recent past, as these are inhibiting factors for the husband who may have problems having or even maintaining an erection. Problems should be resolved early before the couple enters the bedroom for lovemaking. But it does appear that many women like using this opportunity to obtain favors and concessions from their husbands, who, at this critical point, accept to be "good boys" and make promises to please their wives, as long as they have their way.

All the same, the couple may not descend to engaging in wild sexual acts by using their tongues in the "wrong places" through such debasing sexual acts or sodomy as cunnilingus or fellatio usually shown in "blue" movies. As part of the foreplay, a couple should feel free to touch and feel any part of the partner's body, including intimate areas. These actions are intended to put them in the proper mood for the ultimate – sexual intercourse. These days, however, some couples, as part of the foreplay, may decide to switch into *"69 position,"* which is now becoming popular among young and exploring couples. As long as both of them enjoy it, that is okay. These days, too, it is difficult to know what to condemn and what to encourage, as sexual practices/orientations seem to change almost daily, particularly throughout the free world.

A couple should feel free to watch videos that teach good sexual behaviors in an attempt to get a couple to make love, particularly in their waning years or when they do not seem randy enough, when the spirit may be willing, but the body is weak and cannot go along.

The wife should study her husband to know when he is charged (or well aroused) and then let him penetrate in a gradual process before he discharges his "load" elsewhere on her body or on the bed. The man should also study his woman to know when she is ready to receive him. He should then go in gently without being anxious or too eager, lest he discharge his "load" in seconds instead of in minutes. Generally, a man's eagerness to have sex is highest when he is out with a date for the first time. He is eager to "conquer" and establish himself properly with his lady or date.

The couple should feel free to explore and appreciate their bodies through normal or acceptable forms of foreplay. This may include having shower together and washing each other's sex organs, feeding each other in a special way, stroking hair on the chest of the man and a woman's pubic hair, a little bit of "striptease" by the wife for her husband and vice versa, etc. They should choose any position or positions that both of them like, as long as they are not unnecessarily strained and there are no health implications. In this connection, the well-known and age-old "missionary position" (with the man on top) is still a strongly favored position among the young and the old, particularly among beginners and those meeting their partners for the first time. The man should not immediately "dismount" after ejaculating but should remain in the sexual position for at least three minutes, particularly for those looking for a baby. Subject to strain and health, a couple should feel free to try other positions they fancy. Even after disengaging, a couple should still cuddle up and sleep away in heavenly bliss.

Incidentally, it is probably only human beings, among mammals or even in the entire animal kingdom, who have varying or changing sexual positions, according to their whims and caprices. Other animals usually have a genetically coded one-way sexual position. Why human beings are different is difficult to fathom; perhaps, it is because of our genetic makeup, which makes us want to experiment or explore. Whatever sexual position you assume, you should not defy the laws of nature and physics, particularly if you are advanced in age, as you could be seriously hurt.

When randy: What to do

Sometimes a couple feels randy during the day. What is to be done? Nothing, except to go into their room and "express themselves," so long as their children will not come knocking on the door in order to report one thing or the other to their mother or request something. No one can guarantee there will be no knocking on the door when children are at home, except the partners opt for "a quickie." For this and other reasons, married people usually reserve sex for the night when children are supposed to be in bed. In this way, their lovemaking should go on without any interruption.

In this connection, the story is told of a randy couple who was caught red-handed by one of their children. The child, in his innocence and ignorance, pleaded with his father not to "beat" his mother continuously, as the man was busy "pounding away" in the missionary position. The parents had to pretend they were quarrelling, quickly disengaging themselves to attend to the boy's simple request for bread. They had failed to secure their room's door properly in their bid to have a "quick cut" or "quickie."

A similar story is also told of a randy couple who was caught in the act by their child. This time, the couple told their inquisitive child that they were looking for a "playmate brother" for him. The child was quite happy and quickly spread the news among his playmates. The fairly mature ones, who understood that the boy's parents were caught having sex, made jokes out of this.

Parents are, however, advised to be careful and take all necessary precautions in expressing themselves when children are around, especially during the day when all eyes and ears are open. Furthermore, some couples are quite noisy or talkative and occasionally let go some pleasurable shrills or squeals, shouts or words during sexual intercourse. These include such words as: "Darling, go in properly; turn this way and proceed gently; I am enjoying you; you are the best I have ever encountered; I am swimming in pleasure; take me from behind; do not discharge quickly; oh my God; take me to pleasure land," etc. Such shrills or words do attract neighbors and children who are ready to make a jest of the whole episode with their friends. Many men, of course, like such noisy encounters, which seem to heighten their sexual pleasure. Such occasions are better enjoyed when couples are alone and when the room's walls are not porous.

Stealth or mute sex is thus necessary when children are around, when walls or floors are porous or when in-laws of the husband are visiting, as they should not be subjected to sex sounds or movements suggesting some "defilement" of their innocent daughter. This, in some cultures, is disrespectful to in-laws.

Naughty sexual problems

As regards her male partner, a woman should not be put off by the size (length and thickness) of his penis. Her vagina, as highly exaggerated by a well-known female writer on sex matters, "is so wide and freely adjustable that a truck can easily reverse inside." This statement is, of course, hyperbolic, but the point has been well made that a woman's vagina can take any size of penis. Once a woman has been put in the right mood for sex, her vagina will be naturally lubricated to take any size of penis. Without this lubrication, entry by a man is difficult for him and painful to both partners. Men with large or extra large organs should go easy with women and penetrate gently up to a point only, unless their partners are enjoying the whole length and want all of it.

In the same way, a man may be put off by what he finds inside a woman's vagina, which, for instance, may be watery or wet due to excessive lubrication, or by her over-sized breasts. The woman should endeavor to soak up regularly with absorbent tissue paper to enable both of them enjoy sex. Without friction within the vagina (rubbing of the inside walls of the vagina with penis in an up and down motion, as opposed to free floatation), a couple can hardly enjoy sex. Couples should watch out for all these and other inhibiting factors and should therefore eliminate them as far as possible.

Tolerance by both partners is also called for, as no one is born perfect. Until you are intimate with someone, you may not know of any problems, because these are hidden behind smiling faces and well-tailored clothes.

There is no particular time for having sex, but nighttime is usually preferred. Some cultures forbid having sex during the day for various reasons. But young men and women in these societies have cleverly gone around the taboo by creating artificial darkness through drawing down curtains or blinds and closing windows, thus creating a nighttime situation. An alternative may be to drive to a nearby town that has no such taboo, to satisfy their sexual urge. Where, however, couples do not seem to enjoy having sex, they should be forthright and discuss their problems. They should even suggest how sex could be better enjoyed by showing their partners which parts of their bodies or anatomy to touch or fondle, for more effect or sensation. A woman's erotic zones are best known to her. If her husband is not doing enough to arouse her, she should call his attention to this or even move his hand to the areas she wants him to touch. There should be no shyness about this. It is the partner's right. If, after all these measures are taken, a couple is still unsatisfied, counseling by a sex therapist may help. Sex is at the root of all normal marriages. Everything should be explored to ensure that a husband and his wife have a happy and satisfactory sex life.

Lastly, you may be wondering how many times a couple should have sex in a week or month. To a large extent, this depends on the couple. Some couples are more randy than others and may therefore enjoy sex three to four times weekly or even twice daily. Other couples may be content with twice weekly in their early years and once a week as they reach their forties or fifties. But one thing appears certain: interest in sex, with a few exceptions, seems to decrease with advancing age, at which point a wife regards her husband as a big brother or father while a husband regards his wife as a big sister or mother. Of course, nothing stops a couple from enjoying sex in their seventies or eighties, as long as they are physically fit and mentally alert. Men in such age brackets have been known to have children by marrying women young enough to be their grandchildren. If a husband and a wife are not sexually compatible, one of them should be able to adjust upwards or downwards to accommodate the partner. For instance, if the wife likes having sex twice weekly but the husband wants it daily, the wife can accommodate him by managing to go up three or four times weekly. Alternatively, she could stick to her twice-weekly schedule, but should have longer sessions with him once in a while, preferably over weekends when they will be more relaxed.

As the saying goes, too much of anything is bad. Having sex too frequently or infrequently is dangerous to partners. The right balance should be struck. If a man has sex too frequently, he may face protests from his wife, who will tell him that she is not a sex machine. If he stays away from her for long, she may complain that she is being neglected by him. She may even accuse him of having extra marital affairs. Too much of it, he stands accused. Too little of it, he also stands accused. What a paradox! But such is life and there is no escaping this kind of accusation once in a while.

Partners should also try abstinence from sex as a way of mortification, and thus practise what may be imposed on them by circumstances in future. For instance, during some pregnancies, particularly with women who have had a history of miscarriages, doctors may advise total abstinence from sex. This may appear too harsh or too much of a burden for husbands to bear, but it is not too much a sacrifice to make in order to have your own children. Husbands should remember that this sacrifice is just temporary and that in the real world there are many men who have not experienced sex, by choice, and by special circumstances. After all, there are many other ways available for couples to enjoy themselves, feel wanted and loved. All these should then be explored.

Avoiding artificial contraception/abortion

Like other aspects of our lives, couples should bring God and morals into their sexual practices. Artificial contraceptive methods should be shunned as much as possible because there is no natural satisfaction from using them. While safe sex is to be practised, it should exclude the use of artificial contraceptives, as these encourage some people to go for the "real thing" outside marriages, in new relationships, which are by far bigger threats than unwanted pregnancies. Pills damage the body's reproductive system in the long run and could lead to infertility and other health hazards as well. The damage takes a long time to reverse itself. In extreme cases, they prevent conception when couples are ready. Instead, couples should practise natural, preventive methods that help them enjoy their sexual relationship naturally and which teach them the art of abstinence during certain periods, thus bringing more discipline and dignity into their lives. Thus, a couple should work around the wife's menstrual cycle and show more discipline in abstaining from sex during ovulation period, to avoid unwanted pregnancy.

Another problem area is abortion. This, no doubt, is murder, whether the fetus is a day or six months old. Following the Supreme Court ruling in 1973 in the case of Roe vs. Wade, people have apparently accepted, as defined by the Court, that the word "person" as used in the Fourteenth Amendment, does not include the unborn. What a biological, unguarded, and scandalous blunder coming from the highest court in the USA! *Once the egg has been fertilized, a new form of life starts, even if primitive.* All of us went through this process. That is why women who have suffered a natural miscarriage weep because they have lost a developing life. Why should a woman (with the assistance of medical personnel who are supposed to save lives under the Hippocratic Oath) terminate a life she has not created or authored, in a violent and planned manner, with full knowledge of the consequences? This is what lawyers call "premeditation"—the deliberate intention to commit, and actually committing, a crime. A woman and a man knew when they had sex that pregnancy might result. From the time the woman had sex, she waited for one, two, three, four or more months for the "fruit" in her womb to mature before she decided to eliminate it deliberately. This is sheer folly. It is known that some women use pregnancies to lure or entrap men into marriage, but sometimes the plan backfires. This is when women affected think of aborting the pregnancies, totally ignoring danger to their lives. They should have the babies and give them up for adoption. After all, there are many organizations that support such pregnant women, before and after babies are born. Abortion causes a lot of emotional distress, particularly in later years if women involved are unable to become pregnant again. Many modern women unfortunately claim (and are supported by some governments) that they have exclusive right to decide whether to abort or keep their pregnancies. This does not seem right. After all, a pregnancy is the result of sexual liaison between a man and a woman. Both of them should decide the matter, bearing in mind that the man must assume his responsibilities in this regard. In this way, the number of abortions should be significantly reduced.

Women should also understand that having sex or being promiscuous may result in pregnancy and should be careful before sleeping with various shades of men who make heavenly promises and pretend to love them.

Research is still going on about the consequences of abortion on the health of women. It may not be too long before it is realized that unnatural termination of a pregnancy affects the release of hormones and some tissues or organs that had earlier been triggered off at the beginning of the pregnancy, but which have now been disturbed by an abortion. Some research work and some medical personnel seem to support the view that women who have had abortion stand a higher risk of having or developing breast cancer. Even if more research confirms this, many medical practitioners who benefit from abortions will thwart the evidence in order to continue to benefit from this lucrative source of money. So, women should be careful.

The baby a woman intends to abort may be the only one she may ever have, so, why should she abort it? It is far safer and more honorable to carry an unwanted pregnancy to its full term, have the baby, and give it out for adoption, than to engage in an abortion that may cost the life of the woman herself. Doctors who encourage this practice benefit a lot through charging exorbitant fees. Whether you are in school or are about to have a "white wedding," there is nothing to be ashamed of after the deed (having sex) has been done. That is a *fait accompli* (French for *accomplished fact*). That is why many religions insist that there should be no sex before marriage. So, if a woman does not want a pregnancy, she ought to take natural precautions including abstinence from sex. A woman should practise self-control and natural controls that do not harm her body or emotions. If human beings do not respect lives that are just being formed and which cannot defend themselves, what guarantee is there that abortion advocates and other groups will not soon start killing old and terminally sick people, handicapped people, violent criminals, the weak, and sick people carrying infections or contagious diseases in overpopulated countries, in order to make room for healthy people? It may not be long before ungodly people who do not value lives suggest an artificial selection process in a way that "guarantees" the survival of only the fittest or a superhuman race as Adolf Hitler and his henchmen tried to do in Germany during the Second World War (1939-1945). They may even start gene-selection process to eliminate unwanted genes from babies in wombs. It is hoped that such a day never comes, by the special grace of God. Trust humans, they will abuse anything good and try to make money out of it.

Not taking sex life for granted and team work

Husbands and wives should not take their sex lives for granted. The importance of good sexual relationship on a regular basis (as far as health and time permit) is illustrated in the following true story, which took place many years ago. There were two couples (Family A and Family B) living in the same building. The men were railway workers, one a locomotive driver and the other an office worker. The driver usually went on long journeys for many days while his colleague was always at home with his family. Their wives were just housewives with enough time for gossip. The office worker and his wife always had a good time together, particularly at night when the lonely, but alert housewife in the next apartment (with "porous" walls separating them) felt disturbed by the regular "sex bouts" of her neighbors. She was jealous, of course, and wished her own husband were around her at those times. On the return of the driver from his long hauls, the lonely wife would naturally expect her husband's sexual advances, which never came. For days during his off periods, the driver turned his back on his wife, obviously tired from his long journeys. In the meantime, the other couple continued to have a nice time. As time went on, the lonely wife could no longer bear it. In her desire to be faithful to her husband by having only him satisfy her sexually, she summoned up courage. Steadily but gently, she struck her snoring husband in a bid to wake him up. She blurted out the equivalent of these words in her native language: "My son's father! My son's father! Why are you always tired? You always fall asleep too quickly and snore all the way, forgetting that I am by your side. Wake up! Wake up and listen well, you lazy sloth. Listen well to the sounds of sex from our neighbor's apartment and hear how your colleague's penis is pounding away at his wife's vagina. Why don't you do the same thing to me once in a while? I am a woman and I have feelings."

The original language of this text is quite hilarious. Young people in the area and elsewhere who understand the language joke a lot about this incident.

Guess what? Her husband did not respond to all her entreaties that night, as he was too weak and tired, as usual, to follow up and satisfy his wife sexually. Lucky husband! A modern housewife in an urban center with connections and admirers may not have the time or courage to complain about her neglect by her husband. She may seek satisfaction through other sources—orthodox and unorthodox.

Husbands should therefore never take their wives for granted on sex matters; nor should wives their husbands, before wrong steps are regrettably taken. Both groups have sexual feelings.

Furthermore, women should not lose sight of the fact that men are very easily aroused and should be careful how they expose themselves or give wrong signals to their husbands to prepare for sex. If a woman denies her husband sex at a time his sexual urge is high, he may be unhappy for quite some time, which may run into days. So, she should not tease him if she is not ready to "receive" him.

Furthermore, a woman should know that without *adequate teamwork*, both of them will not enjoy sex. She should therefore throw away all inhibitions and give her husband some helping hand by making gyratory movements in unison or harmony with the man's movements. She should not lie down or take a position like dead wood or a log and expect her husband to do all the "work." As her husband gets older, he needs more help to get him properly aroused and retain erection for as long as each sex session lasts.

Lastly, partners should avoid all remarks or unnatural actions on their part that inhibit erection or enjoyment of sex once they agree to have sex.

All human beings are products of sex. They should all endeavor to preserve its respectability or dignity and enjoy it the way nature intended from the beginning of mankind.

May people's sex lives continue to *spark*! May couples avoid infidelity, homosexuality and other forms of sexual behavior that debase humanity, marriage, and the family unit!

Highlights

Sex between loved ones is beautiful.

Inhibiting factors should be recognized and removed as much as possible.

Men and women, particularly men, cannot have their way all the time.

People should enjoy sex with loved ones only. Sex with any other persons may be dangerous to their health. This surgeon-general-like warning should actually be observed by all married people, if not by all adults.

Partners should understand each other's sex needs and adjust accordingly.

No group—men or women—should be taken for granted on sex matters.

Abortion should be ruled out at all times. It is murder, pure and simple. A fetus is the beginning of life and should not be destroyed deliberately.

Sex problems between partners should be discussed with all sincerity and seriousness, without any inhibitions whatsoever.

Chapter 10

Bringing up Children

"Today's adults and leaders were yesterday's children. Today's children will be tomorrow's adults and leaders. So, let us bring them up properly as children of God and good citizens through good education, culture, hard work, respect for life, good manners, and observance of the law in order to have more responsi - ble citizenry."

Social stigma where there are no children

Children are one of the fruits and blessings of marriage in virtually all parts of the world. In those regions where children are considered a must in a relationship, there is, sometimes, discrimination between sexes of children. Obviously, girls are more expensive and delicate to bring up than boys. They are also exposed to more risks than boys. Thus, many couples tend to prefer boys to girls for no justifiable reasons whatsoever, except those embedded in antiquated beliefs and cultures under which men want male children who will perpetuate family names and bring "honor" in other spheres of life. Even the fact that some women now answer their maiden names after marriage or combine them with their husbands' names does not satisfy some male chauvinists. In these same cultures, adoption of children is usually unknown or frowned upon since children of relations are always available to be taken care of. The reasoning here seems to be: "Why adopt children from outside extended families when there are enough nephews, nieces, cousins, etc., to be assisted?"

In this regard, if a couple does not have a child within a year of marriage, tongues of relations start carrying gossip around about apparent infertility of the wife or other assumed problems. If nothing still happens after another year or pro-longed period, the innocent wife may be kicked out by angry in-laws and told in clear terms that her husband could not live with "another man." This approach, to say the least, is usually humiliating for the wife. The real problem may even lie with the husband, who may have low sperm count, among other equally serious problems. But illiterate people never think that there could be such a problem, which to them is not possible. They think the problem is unlikely to exist. They have probably never heard of low sperm count or erectile dysfunction in its various forms. Happily, with education and religious teaching, many people are beginning to realize that a marriage need not be severed because there are no children. Sometimes, through no fault of theirs, a couple may not have children early in their relationship, despite night after night of trying very hard. Sometimes, these frequent acts of lovemaking become frustrating if the wife does not report that she has missed her period. They become gloomy. They then start to think that it is a waste of time having sex with a view to starting a family. However, they need not think so, as God's time is the best. They should just continue to try. It is not unknown that a couple who could not have children in their first fifteen years of marriage started having them later. Furthermore, some couples may have children in the early years and have a gap of up to seven years or more before other children arrive. There may be nothing wrong with them except perhaps bad luck in the timing of their lovemaking.

Even ordinary anxiety to have children can stop a wife from becoming pregnant and cause her a lot of stress; so a couple having problems with pregnancy should do well to consult a good gynecologist and also pray hard for God's intervention before in-laws and relations start gossiping about them.

Sometimes, too, in many Western societies, some couples may decide to get married and not have any children at all. So the choice is yours to make, but be sure to explain your intentions to your loved one and any others before marriage, so that gossips are not carried around about you.

Number of children for a couple

As regards the number of children a couple would like to have, economic difficulties of the twentieth and twenty-first centuries and inconveniences parents undergo make it almost mandatory for them to decide early how many children to have. Surprisingly, in many developed countries, many couples simply decide not to have children, leading to negative population growth or seriously declining population after some years. This is dangerous, as people who are aging and dying are not being replaced in those countries.

In some countries that are highly overpopulated, the law limits the number to one child. Although there are occasional violations that are punished in various ways, the main reason for this limitation is to avoid very serious overpopulation and its consequences on available space, social amenities and food resources. Remember that if population is unchecked, the tendency is for it to multiply by *geometric proportions* particularly in developing countries where family planning is almost nonexistent, while food supplies increase only by *arithmetic proportions*. This idea was probably first postulated by **Rev. Thomas Robert Malthus**, a classical economist and clergyman, who lived from 1766 to 1834. He had argued then that the population of the world tended to increase faster than food supplies and that without birth control in place, war and poverty would serve as a natural restriction of the increase. How true if you care to look around the world! Furthermore, due to great advances in medicine and technology, people seem to live longer now than they did previously. Thus, by the time people say "Jack Robinson," they may be bumping into themselves in the near future, as they now almost do in many megacities of the world—Tokyo, London, New York, Lagos, Mexico City, etc.

Watch films of high-density cities around the world and see how people move in city centers and along busy highways, like packed sardines. See how people occupy and fight for every available space! Many couples many years ago did not have major distractions from television or movies and so had all the time in the world to rely on a cheap and readily available source of fun—sex. The cost has been quite high in terms of population explosion and dwindling or depleting natural resources that cannot go around.

In some countries, it has since been realized that a two-child family is ideal. Some people have therefore adjusted to this trend which is gradually catching up in many Third World countries that have overpopulation problems. With advances in medical science, improvements in living conditions and progress in social justice throughout the world—all of which have contributed significantly toward longer life expectancy—the need for a large family apparently no longer exists. Largely gone are the days when couples depended on children to help them with farm work or make contributions toward the family income. Many children these days, unfortunately, are barely able to look after themselves, even after graduating from college. As adults, some of them continue to depend on their parents for financial support. This, to say the least, is quite regressive.

Each couple should therefore decide how many children they want and when to have them. They should bear in mind that after age thirty-five or thereabouts, a woman finds it increasingly difficult to bear the burdens of pregnancy and childbirth.

The financial condition of each couple should be considered, as well as any applicable laws and the need to bring up children while the parents are still young, resourceful and strong. Thus, children should be able to support themselves by the time their parents reach middle ages—fifty five to sixty—to enable them retire early from active work without serious financial strains.

This also brings up again the question of early marriage to enable people achieve goals they have set for themselves. Perhaps, the ideal age for a man to get married is between twenty six and thirty while a woman's ideal age is between twenty four and twenty six, giving her enough time to have two to three children before she is thirty five. Exceptionally, through no fault of theirs, some women continue to bear children while they are in their late thirties or early forties. They should recognize the risk they face and ensure they receive good medical attention and conserve their energy for "labor day." Parents-to-be should also remember that the burden of bringing up children increases from year to year. Among expenses to consider are school bills, medical/domestic bills, and, where applicable, nanny/child-care payments, etc.

Preparing to have children

Having children is a pleasant experience. Parents should therefore be prepared to welcome them. If they are not ready to do so (and being ready means ability and willingness to sacrifice time, personal liberties, and material resources for their happiness and well being), they should postpone having them or decide not to have them at all.

Assuming a couple decides to have children, the wife should, <u>inter alia:</u>

See a good gynecologist early enough in the pregnancy in order to receive proper advice, examination, and medication.

Buy some books on women matters including pregnancies, in order to have good grounding in developments of the pregnancy and what she herself can or cannot do during this period.

Buy all things necessary for the baby as the due date approaches.

Assemble or gather every thing she needs to take to the hospital or maternity home at a moment's notice, including cash for emergency use.

Make good provision for transportation to the hospital, including arrangements with neighbors, if necessary, when labor pains set in.

Arrange for proper care of grownup children in her absence.

Ensure there is phone in the house.

Have emergency and other numbers handy.

To further prepare herself for pregnancy and child birth, a wife is advised to buy a good book on these subject matters so as to familiarize herself with what happens in all phases of pregnancy:

Child movements

Exercises to take (with approval of her doctor)

Foods to take

Things to avoid (including sex if advised to do so by the doctor)

Signs of labor pains, including false signs

Hygiene during pregnancy and after child birth, etc.

She should be ready to question her doctors and nurses about procedures that are to be adopted and, if necessary, opt for procedures which will make her more comfortable. She should remember that some medical personnel sometimes make mistakes and that she should be alert because her life is involved. Many women are alive today because they were alert during child birth and pointed out wrong procedures to those attending to them.

Before delivery, you should familiarize yourself with baby care in at least these areas, among others:

Feeding procedures (breast and/or feeding bottle) and expelling wind after each feed

Hygiene maintenance of self, baby, and surroundings

Safety for baby
Cleaning/washing of baby
Sleeping and keeping watch
Signs to observe for illness or discomfort and what to do.

Where you are not sure what to do, ask your doctor or nurse or even call and ask your mother or neighbors. They will be too eager and happy to help; so do not feel shy to ask someone for help if you have a problem.

As your child grows up, you, as a mother, have the major responsibility of monitoring your child to ensure he/she is growing and behaving normally and to report any problems or suspicions to an expert for professional evaluation. You handle the baby more than anybody else, hence you have this responsibility. Looking after a baby is always a fulltime job, but only a few men and women realize this.

By this time, the husband should be very close to the wife to help in any emergency. However, if for any reasons he has to be away, adequate arrangement must be made with a relation or friend to be with her until she fully recovers after safe delivery. In the "good old days," this was where the wife's mother or mother-in-law or an elderly close relation fitted in almost perfectly, as she also helped with domestic chores while the nursing mother rested or recuperated.

Arrival of children is celebrated formally in some cultures through name giving after a number of days ranging from, say, eight to twenty-eight days. Feasting and special prayers for mothers and children accompany such ceremonies. In some other cultures and circumstances, parents wait for the children to be baptized or initiated into the parents' religions before feasting takes place. Obviously, since mothers have gone through excruciating and life-threatening labor pains, safe delivery deserves special thanksgiving and celebration. Whichever course of action parents decide upon, they should show moderation and stay within their resources.

Another area to watch is circumcision of children. Most males get circumcised in virtually all cultures, while that of females is gradually dying out, as a lot of mutilation of the female sex organ is involved, in the name of circumcision and the need to make girls feel less randy or easily stimulated or sexy. Mothers should also ensure that their male children do not have erectile dysfunction. They should check that the penis stands erect or is at least partially erect when boys are urinating. If it is otherwise, doctors should be consulted early.

Bringing up children and essentials of life

Ideally, children should be brought up in a loving atmosphere, under the influence of both parents. Generally, a father tends to be very strict and rigid while a mother is usually soft, shows more understanding with children, and is more flexible with them. She also listens carefully to them to understand their problems. Even adults are usually treated or regarded as toddlers by their mothers. Women generally do not believe that their children, even as adults, can fend for themselves and are always willing to advise them and even supervise their day-to-day activities.

Until their last day on earth, their maternal instinct will always be aroused to ensure that their children have adequate protection and enough food to keep body and soul together. The same mothers, through this maternal instinct, are also willing to lay down their lives for their children's sake. A mother's love for her children knows no bounds.

The dual care by parents ensures that children have a balanced upbringing, under which they have neither been pampered nor ill-treated nor abused. Thus a father uses the "stick" while a mother uses the "carrot" to get children to comply with what is socially acceptable. Sometimes, it is the other way around—a father using the carrot and a mother using the stick. Thus, it should not be all stick or all carrot. A mixture ensures this balanced upbringing.

Even if one of the parents is away for a good reason, the other parent can carry on alone but should report what has happened to the partner, who can then phone or write to support the partner looking after the children. The unity of parents in this respect is important, otherwise wrong signals will be sent to the children—that one parent is very harsh and bad while the other is lenient and good. There will then be a tendency for the children to hate the harsh parent and carry this hatred with them throughout life. Even if a couple disagrees on this, they can sort the matter out in privacy and reach a compromise.

In bringing up children, couples should remember what St. Paul advised in his Epistle to the Ephesians 6: 4

Fathers, do not provoke your children to anger, but bring them up in the discipline and instruction of the Lord.

Children are innocent of their actions, utterances, and dangers in their surroundings. Children play with all objects without knowing the dangers inherent in them. Children dismantle all objects they can reach with a view to satisfying their curiosity as to the contents. Even when a parent and his child are hiding from an enemy, particularly during a war, the child in all his innocence may cry out without knowing the danger they have been exposed to. There is nothing one can do about it except to pray that one is not discovered and then try to soothe the child by offering breast milk, food, or water.

No one should take advantage of children, abuse them, or mislead them. Abuse takes various forms ranging from depriving children of reasonable care and upkeep to hurting them and carelessly exposing them to danger.

God's anger awaits any person who seriously deviates from this St. Paul's advice. As the Lord Jesus Christ said in one of his teachings, "It is to them that the kingdom of God belongs."

Children should be taught everything around them at the right time: learning various cultures that influence them directly and other cultures and peoples. They should be taught simple morals. They should be told about laws they should respect and obey and the consequences of not being law abiding, people and places to avoid, how to use facilities around them, and, above all, how to take care of themselves and their surroundings. They should be taught to love, appreciate, praise, tell the truth and keep to time. They should also be taught to work hard, eat good food, and help in the house and in the community they live in. At the other end, they should be taught not to discriminate, hate or be violent, tell lies or condemn without good reasons in some circumstances.

They should be given some leadership and survival training within youth movements and other appropriate organizations. This will help them, as they grow up, to face the harsh realities of life, whether in a rural or an urban setting. Furthermore, they should be told who their relations are, where they come from, and their expectations in life at the appropriate times. They should be taught how to cope with life in difficult times and that the world is not exactly a bed of roses. They should learn to perform all domestic chores including cooking, so that they do not have to depend on anyone or buy junk food all the time. Whether rich or poor, parents must teach their children all essential basics of life, so that they do not go astray at any time. They should never be spoiled; otherwise they may never make it on their own later in life. Then parents have nobody but themselves to blame for overpampering their children.

Disciplining children

As regards applying discipline on children, the old saying "spare the rod and spoil the child" should always be remembered. There are laws in many countries that protect children from parental and other abuses. These are heavily and sometimes recklessly enforced in these countries without due regard to the bond or relationship between parents and children. There are apparently no laws under which children are punished or reprimanded when they disobey parents or fail to conform to certain norms or even assist in doing simple domestic chores. The result is that many children are spoiled and carry this into adulthood and eventually graduate into "big time" criminals or irresponsible citizens.

Children have to be "bent" like the twig tree, as early as possible because this is what a happy and prosperous life entails. As part of their training, children should be cautioned or rebuked where this is required and punished for disobedience and other lapses. This will constantly remind them that there are laws and conditions governing our lives and actions, if there must be discipline and respect for other people's rights in society. Thus, they may pay fines and/or face jail terms if there are serious breaches of the law when they become adults. These days, of course, many countries and states try children less than eighteen years old as adults if the former commit heinous crimes such as murder.

Punishment for children these days in some countries may take the form of restricting them from watching favorite television programs or asking them to go to their bedrooms or just giving them a serious reprimand. Sometimes, the punishment may take the simple form of writing out an apology or imposition ("I shall never do this again" or something similar) up to, say, fifty times. These forms of punishment may be regarded as "modern" or "civilized" (even if apparently inadequate) in order not to violate civil laws regarding treatment and abuse of children and the underprivileged. In other countries, punishment takes much more serious forms, in order to force children to comply with set norms. This includes corporal punishment (strokes of the cane or horsewhip), pulling at the cheeks and/or ears, hand strokes on the buttocks, sending them to do farm work or domestic chores, trimming flowers or mowing grass, denial of favorite food or drink, or a good combination of these. In some very serious situations, some parents report the matter to school authorities, who may have to discipline children involved before the school assembly and their parents. Of course, in all of this, no injury is intended or should be inflicted.

However, where children have excelled or done extraordinary things, they should be praised or rewarded with candy or special gifts during festivities. But this should not be overdone, to avoid inviting pomposity and arrogance from children.

Parents should not give children all they ask of them. They have to learn the harsh realities of life early—that one cannot always get what one wants without a price or cost to consider. You cannot eat your cake and have it at the same time. Nothing is really free. Someone has to pay for it, one way or another. They have to be taught how to make real choices that will benefit them in the long run. Even if you are superfluously rich, you should not spoil your children by giving them what they cannot maintain or appreciate, as this may be equivalent to "throwing pearls to swine." Children's lives should be moderated so that in difficult times, they can cope without resorting to stealing or doing other mean things such as selling or using drugs, organizing sex shows, or being involved in prostitution or pimping work. If their parents are involved with some form of handiwork, they should assist them periodically, so as to ensure their daily bread is available. It should be a joy to assist one's parents in whatever way one can, but children never realize this until much later in life.

Children should be taught humility; respect for other people's views; respect and love for the sick, the deprived and the elderly; and, above all, the love and fear of God to whom everyone is accountable for all thoughts, omissions, and actions.

If parents can afford it, their children should go to the best schools, as a sound education is the best legacy parents can bestow on their children, not physical or material wealth. Knowledge is mightier than wealth, just as the pen is mightier than the sword. Where parents cannot afford good schools for their children and the latter are compelled to go to lower quality schools, private teachers could be engaged to help them during weekends or long holidays. Children should also be given time to study by themselves. This habit should be developed early before they go to college or university, where they will virtually be on their own. Among other things, children should be taught to use public transportation in case of emergencies such as when the family's car breaks down. They should know how to pick their special friends who share the same or positive values and drop those who are a negative influence on them. Parents should also take note of those people their children talk to on telephone or through the Internet so as to guide them properly.

Regular medical examination for them up to high-school age is recommended so that any health problems will be addressed early before they go to college. In this connection, using a regular pediatrician or general practitioner ensures that children's medical history is handy for reference at all times.

Teaching children sex matters

While children are always welcome, there are many things parents should not do in their presence. They should remember that children learn to imitate and mimic adults. Expectedly, bad habits and practices are easy to copy. So, parents should not engage in any fighting, serious quarrels, passionate kissing, or cuddling in the presence of their children, as these are bound to arouse their children's interest and they may soon practise them with their mates. Gossiping, watching X-rated films, and reading adult magazines in the presence of underage children should be avoided. One good thing, though, is that parents generally refrain from discussing sex matters in detail with, or reading adult magazines in the presence of, their children.

When children raise questions about sex, parents should be diplomatic in their answers, telling them in strong terms that as they get older, they will learn more about sex. And more they will certainly learn from their mates, biology lessons, and films, just as the adults did in their youth. Parents have never been known to be at ease or free to discuss intimate sexual matters with their children. Fortunately or unfortunately, when teenagers have questions about sex, their mothers are usually the first they ask. Women, with a few exceptions, have never been known to do a good job of discussing detailed sex matters with, of all people, their children.

While they are growing up, children should be taught to respect the opposite sex and value their contributions to the procreation process and humanity in general. In this way, as they mature into adults, they will appreciate these valuable lessons and learn to be good spouses.

Parents should not run themselves down in the presence of their children, as they will soon learn to show their dislike for the run-down partner. This tends to militate against discipline within a home.

Children should be encouraged to speak out when they have problems and to go to their parents or other relations when their advice is needed. It is the moral duty of parents and guardians to give advice to their children, even those above eighteen years, thus satisfying their conscience. It is a different matter whether they take the advice or not.

Lastly, as soon as children are of age, say twenty-one and above, they should *learn* to be on their own, except they are still in college or have serious handicap. Where they decide to live on their own, children should not be told how to perform day-to-day activities, including management of their lives; otherwise, they may run away from their parents who they consider to be all controlling. Parents should talk to them like adults and let them see the good and bad sides of planned actions. The choice is theirs to make. They soon learn from their mistakes, just as mature adults did.

As gifts of nature, children should be well guided and guarded, as nothing is more precious than these little ones. Our Lord Jesus said something similar in the Bible when he preached that the kingdom of God belonged to these little ones.

Highlights

Children are a blessing and should be welcomed at all times.

They should be brought up in a balanced manner, using the carrot and the stick approach. They should be taught how to face life's problems realistically.

They should be given proper education about their cultural background, surroundings, and other matters that influence or endanger their lives.

Children should be disciplined appropriately, to remind them that laws and morals govern our lives and that we face the consequences if and when we deviate.

Parents should decide early whether or not they want children, and the number, bearing in mind applicable laws and other factors such as ability to love and raise them properly.

Parents should put up good behavior before their children at all times.

Children should be allowed to grow up and learn from their mistakes, as long as such mistakes are not life threatening or too costly.

Chapter 11
Understanding Your Partner's Career or Job

"Knowing what your partner does outside the home creates a better atmosphere within the home and leads to a better understanding of your partner's behavior."

Need to know mate's routines

To reduce or avoid any serious misunderstandings in your relationship, it is necessary to understand the kind of work your partner does. This will help you appreciate any issues being raised about the job, discuss problems, and offer advice as appropriate.

Some people have special talents and have also received special training that they would not like to waste by staying idle. They also need to support the family, and help others and further develop their talents. If, therefore, a wife has these attributes, it may be difficult for her husband to convince her to stay at home and face the home front. In these days of economic hardship and other uncertainties surrounding even fulltime jobs, a wife should be there to render some support to her family. She should also be able to carry on the family burden alone, if necessary, when the main breadwinner is no longer in a position to do so.

Thus, knowing your spouse's routines in the office or even at home helps to expand your areas of communication with each other, as well as knowing their colleagues, bosses, office locations, phone numbers, movements during office hours, and even some of their clients, without giving away business secrets. In some situations, a partner may even help with jobs brought home for completion. Where a partner is on vacation or is available, arrangements can be made for both of them to attend seminars or other official functions together, thus further cementing the relationship.

To work or not to work

In the early years of a relationship, there may be the need to raise children. Should the wife then take up an outside job while children are being raised or stay at home until all children have reached school age? Should she combine working with raising children? Remember that raising children is quite a big and fulltime job from which you cannot remove your eyes, even for a minute, except when they are asleep. Can the family afford to employ a nanny or housekeeper? Can a maid be trusted to look after children who are just developing? Is the wife's income a major part of the total family income that the family cannot afford to forgo? Has a child any traits, disabilities, symptoms or other health problems that require special attention from a loving parent?

These and similar questions are for the couple to answer, taking into consideration the pros and cons of each issue. The same questions can be raised in respect of the husband whose income may be far lower than his wife's. In this case, will the husband be willing to stay at home and look after children while his wife works? Will he be willing to take care of domestic chores such as doing dishes, cleaning the house, cooking, and doing laundry, among other chores that are traditionally meant for wives? Is he willing to clean up children when they mess up? If the experience of married people is anything to go by, only husbands who are driven to the wall may be willing to become "househusbands," if at all, and they are *very few*. One reason for this attitude may be that men have not been designed by nature or brought up by their parents to stay at home, take care of domestic chores, and look after children. Nature generally designed women with the entire wherewithal and maternal instinct, including patience and tolerance, to look after children. Any other arrangement (with men) will last for only a short while.

If it becomes necessary for the wife to stay at home, it must be ensured that adequate insurance policies are taken out on the lives of both partners or on the husband's life at least. This is to ensure the ability of a partner to cope, in case of any mishap such as death or a major disability. Even if the wife becomes a fulltime housewife for the time being, she can keep herself busy by writing, doing home study, learning to use the computer, or doing some gardening, among a number of things in her spare time. Her husband should not forget to take her out as regularly as possible so that she does not feel bored and start to complain that she has been neglected.

Where both partners decide to work, a number of matters should be considered, in the interest of the children and overall family welfare. A partner can work during the day and the other partner at night, so that the children have one of the parents with them at all times. A concerned husband or wife may ask how both of them could ever fulfill their sexual obligations if they never stay at home together. To this, the simple answer is that both of them just have to find time, one way or another, to have sexual relations, even if it is a "quickie." During holidays, vacation or weekends, they can always make up.

Where necessary, a lower paying job may be taken up, in the interest of the children. Remember that in normal circumstances, no one can take care of children better than the parents themselves. Location of schools for children, choice of residence, and transportation issues can significantly influence where parents decide to go for jobs. Thus, if you do not have a car, you should look for a job that does not take you too far away from home, all things considered.

Lastly, when it comes to the question of transferring to another job or changing locations such as moving to another state or country, your partner should be involved in this decision making process. Both parents and children will be affected by any decision taken. The possible implications or impact may be too much for one partner alone to comprehend. If things do not work out well as envisioned, a partner should look for another job and stay with the family, as relocation can be expensive and also disruptive for children, and even adults. Sometimes, decisions are difficult to make, but remember that the welfare of the family is paramount.

Where your job involves traveling out of town or meeting often with members of the opposite sex, you should take your partner into confidence by letting him or her have some details of such meetings and those involved, as long as security matters or confidentiality are not breached. This advice should also go down well with actors and actresses who now see it fit to invite their spouses to film locations when sexual acts are to be performed. While only partners with nerves should watch, this approach helps to build up a lasting trust. However, one still wonders why producers or directors of movies introduce highly amorous and explosive raw sex scenes into movies, scenes involving even married actors and actresses. Simulated sex scenes should be okay to satisfy audiences. No wonder the rate and the frequency of divorce among these people are extremely high, and, of course, extremely expensive and disruptive of lives!

In this connection, dangerous liaisons or situations in which your actions may be misunderstood should be avoided, as these may lead to marital problems. It is good to inform your partner early where such situations have arisen or are likely to arise. Furthermore, it is good to have witnesses in case their testimony is required in future. Your actions should be fully explained. In this way, you should have full support from your partner, as long as the whole truth and nothing but the truth has been told.

Partners ought to learn from what has happened to other people. Instead, regrettably, the same mistakes (sometimes worse) are repeated, forgetting that their lives are an open book if they depend on public patronage for their livelihood and if they are civil or public servants.

Avoiding sexual harassment situations

It is also necessary to mention **sexual harassment** matters that are now being given prominence in many parts of the world. These have taken a different dimension from what they used to be, particularly in some developed countries. Defining sexual harassment is becoming more and more difficult, as what is regarded as sexual harassment in one country may mean nothing in another country or state.

By way of refreshing one's memory, sexual harassment in days gone-by was limited to the use of violent attack or excessive force to obtain sexual favors from members of the opposite sex without their free and continuous consent. It was mostly limited to men who forced women, under various kinds of threats, to have sex with them, sometimes even at knife, blade, or scissors point. Thus, there was no free consent on the part of the women. Even at that, husbands, it was rightly or wrongly assumed, could not rape their wives as long as the women were not threatened with any weapons and as long as they lived under the same roof with their husbands. Rape was probably the only sexual crime that was well known and well defined, particularly where there had been penile penetration of the vagina.

IN SOME COUNTRIES, SOME JUDGES AND LAWYERS EVEN WENT ON TO ARGUE THAT RAPE INVOLVED 100 PER CENT OR FULL PENETRATION, NOT FIFTY PER CENT OR THE MERE TOUCHING OF THE VAGINA WITH PENIS. This was really ridiculous, as measuring the exact percentage of penetration was extremely difficult. Should a rape victim be used as a guinea pig for this measurement? This would be adding insult to injury. The problem really was the way the law defined rape. Attorneys for both sides would always look for a way to have the law on their side. Monetary compensation at that time for the sexually harassed was outside the question. Employers were never involved in the matter. It was just between the accused and the accuser in "you said this or that or I did this or that situation." With no DNA testing available at the time, many rapists were lucky to escape justice.

These days, a sexual harassment charge has taken a new turn and has even gone "nuclear." Men and women can be accused, even though men are by far in the majority—in fact, over 90 percent of all cases. Merely telling a female office colleague or a neighbor that she is beautiful and has a good figure can invite trouble for the man or admirer. Usually, a harassment charge is made by a subordinate against a supervisor or superior officer, but never the other way around. These days, too, the accused may include a few deranged or misguided priests. Usually, too, the accused is rich and has influence and should be in a position to make substantial monetary compensation to the accuser. Employers are also involved and penalized where it is determined that they ignored reports or looked the other way and did nothing to stop the harassment.

If the accused is a pauper or has no influence, nothing usually happens thereafter. The matter is allowed to lie low, or be in the doldrums for long, or even entirely forgotten. But this is not so if the accused is rich or has influence, including churches, even if the accusation is highly exaggerated or false. The whole world must hear it.

What actually is sexual harassment? Does it include mere expression of admiration or actual request for sexual liaison or refusal to grant someone his or her right such as promotion or a raise in the office unless there is sexual liaison? Must there be sexual undertone in any harassment matters? Males could harass males while females could harass females without any sex being involved. In these situations (and even in some cases involving the opposite sex), a superior officer can still harass a subordinate if he or she does not like the staff. This can be done through undue criticisms of output, manner of dressing, and asking the subordinate to perform unpleasant tasks while those he or she likes are scored highly and given light duties. In these instances, it is usually difficult to prove any harassment.

What then should be said or not be said to the opposite sex, to avoid being accused of sexual harassment? How then does a man convey his feelings to a woman whom he admires, if he wants to date or marry her? Don't women enjoy flattery anymore? Don't they want to be admired by men any longer? Will this "fear" not drive men "underground" and isolate women, particularly the highly educated ones? Only women have these answers.

Future sexual harassment scenarios

Society has now gone from using brute or excessive force to using verbal expressions in defining sexual harassment. Perhaps, in the near future in this fast paced world of ours, merely looking at a woman (beautiful or ugly, as in the eyes of the beholder) as she passes by may invite accusation of sexual harassment. As is well known, the eyes send messages to those who can read such messages effectively. Even the hands can be used to send messages across without someone actually talking. Vulgar sign "language," which cannot be heard but can be seen and "interpreted" by those who understand the language can be used to send messages to the opposite sex.

Where then can the line be drawn? After all, the woman also looked at the man; if she did not, how did she know that he was looking at her? In any case, how can it be determined that the man started looking at her first, or was it the other way around? If a woman succeeds in nailing down a man for merely looking at her (and this is not impossible judging from the rate at which society is going), then society should be ready for the next stage in this sexual harassment war. This will be when a woman accuses a man of harboring sexual feelings toward her, judging from the man's behavior such as continuously staring at her, whether in admiration or contempt. This will be the ultimate war between the sexes and perhaps the beginning of the end of sexual liaison between men and women!

All this is not to say that women are not harassed sexually on a regular basis. However, let women nip the problem in the bud by politely declining sexual overtures from those they do not approve and reporting subsequent overtures to appropriate authorities. If, for instance, a man stares at a lady, she should look another way rather than confront him. They should try to distinguish serious from nonserious cases and understand that men, by nature, are bound to admire them and pass some positive comments about their bodies. In some societies, if men embarrass women by talking lewdly to them, women also retaliate, and, in time, the men respect themselves and keep quiet. Both sides sometimes enjoy these lewd talks as long as they are jokes. They help to relieve tension and boredom. They also help in understanding the minds of both sexes.

So, if you are influential, occupy a high position in public or private enterprise, or are rich, you should watch your words and weigh them carefully when you talk to members of the opposite sex. Your best bet is to keep your mouth shut and avoid trouble and embarrassment. If you do not keep your mouth shut, you may lose your job. Some of your properties may also go to the accuser. Even if you are poor and do not occupy any high position, your best bet is to keep your mouth shut to avoid losing your job.

The odds are that society has not yet heard the last about developments in this matter of sexual harassment.

People learn every day. Laws and ways of life also change every day.

Highlights

Understand your partner's career or job, so as to better appreciate each other.

Take your partner into confidence when changing jobs and consider the welfare of your entire family.

Decide how your children can be taken care of if both of you work.

Avoid sexual harassment situations.

Inform your partner if you deal with the opposite sex a lot and where there are likely to be any problems, in order to obtain necessary support.

Chapter 12

Planning Your Future Together

"Plan your future in order to ensure reasonable happiness and ability to cope with problems when they arise. Not planning to succeed indirectly means planning to fail or accepting failure as an option."

Reasons for planning

Many young people and even some elderly ones do not usually think about their future, let alone make plans. They tend to take life more leisurely, each day at a time, in the false hope that tomorrow will take care of itself. It is doubtful if tomorrow will always take care of itself in today's world where brotherly love is fast disappearing and where selfishness and greed are more visible. Since there is no law anywhere in the world against selfishness and greed, many people will continue to be selfish and greedy. In fact, it is extremely difficult, if not impossible, to define these terms. Try defining them and you end up being more confused. It is, perhaps, your mind that will make you feel that you have reached a point where you should share whatever you have with friends, neighbors and all others; that you have much more than you will actually require in a lifetime.

The world is moving and changing at a pace many people cannot understand or cope with. It is therefore sheer foolhardiness to follow this approach of not planning. There are just too many uncertainties in life these days to leave certain things or even anything to chance, without planning with available resources and information from all possible sources.

Without going into details, it is well known that without plans people will simply grope in the dark or drift along. But with plans, no matter their imperfections, people are able to avoid major pitfalls and manage any problems on the tortuous journey of life. Just as businesses and other organizations plan their operations and profits to eliminate major pitfalls and ensure success, couples should also plan their lives together. Even social misfits such as drug dealers, armed robbers, thieves, kidnappers, or rapists meticulously plan their operations and invariably pray before embarking on their trips in order to minimize mistakes and ensure "success." This so-called success is equivalent to a "Pyrrhic victory or success" for the perpetrators because such actions are socially, morally, and legally unacceptable. They are costly in terms of human lives that may be involved, cost of property lost, and the serious trauma to the victims, if the latter are fortunate to be alive. Making plans for your future is good and should be cultivated, no matter how crude they are.

Planning helps you compare what is on the ground with your plan, thus enabling you to make changes as necessary to achieve your goals or objectives.

Matters to consider

As soon as a couple settles down after tedious wedding activities, they should seriously discuss and pay attention to a number of issues that are crucial to their happiness. Some of these can be handled immediately while others can be attended to in future, as the occasions arise. These include, but are not limited to:

> Number of children they would like to have.
> Education for the children and higher education/professional training for the couple
> Ownership of residential accommodation, land, stocks, etc.
> Savings, insurance policies, and other investments
> Extended family obligations, if any
> Activities in retirement.
> Traveling and leisure activities
> Health matters and periodic medical check ups
> Family visits and reunions

There is really no time to waste because the earlier both partners start the process, the better the result and the happier they will be, all things remaining equal. You and your spouse do not have all the time in the world to do all these. Remember that each person lives an average of seventy to eighty years; that is, if you are lucky to escape being killed violently on the streets of New Orleans or Detroit or dying through an Al-Qaeda-type sponsored terrorism anywhere in the world. So make up your mind and start implementing your plans for a bright future.

The number of children to be had depends on both of you --your health, economic resources now and in future, laws in force, religious inclination, and other factors. Remember that breast milk is the best and that a baby should be breast-fed for at least six months in order to properly cement the bond between mother and child and for the health of the baby. If a wife has to spend all her income paying a nanny to look after her child, she may as well stay at home unless her job holds great future potentials for her.

As regards education for children, you have to decide early the kind of school you want them to attend—public, private, a mixture of both or a religious school run by missionaries. You obviously want the best for your children, within your resources, in such a way that academic, civic, or moral education and values are combined in the best proportions. If one area is missing, you have to provide your children with it outside the school system, perhaps in a Sunday school. They need not go to expensive schools in order to have good education. Like you do window-shopping for clothes, cars, and other goods and services, you should look around to see what suits your children and your pocket.

In connection with residential accommodation, do you want to be a tenant for life? For a rational person, all things remaining equal, the answer is obviously no, except one's income is so low that the necessary conditions cannot be met. Even then, at old age when income from various sources tends to dry up, how will you settle your rentals? This makes it imperative for you to plan toward having a home, no matter how small, unfashionable, or distant from the city center, as long as it meets planning and developmental laws. What is more, landed properties tend to appreciate in value from year to year, except in areas that are prone to natural disasters or economic depression. If you cannot afford any house from your income, perhaps you should approach mortgage finance institutions and see how you fit into their program. Perhaps you may be required to save regularly with them, as your ultimate goal is to get a house, a town home, or a condominium. Even buying an undeveloped plot of land could be a good starting point. The time to start is now, not tomorrow, at least for the sake of your children. You should leave something for them if you can.

Do both of you like to travel round the country or the world during vacations? Do you enjoy traveling to exotic places? How else would you wish to spend your leisure time—reading, playing games, gardening, writing, watching television, attending parties, performing community service, or helping out in charitable institutions? Do you simply want to enjoy old age in a rocking chair, sitting around the fire place to pipe away or read junk magazines, if they keep you happy?

What of your extended or larger families on both sides? How do you intend to help out, remembering that you were perhaps their major breadwinner before your marriage? If you have younger ones in college, how do you intend to assist them until they can stand on their feet? What of your aged parents? Will putting them in a retirement home wreck them psychologically or emotionally? Instead, is it better to provide them with live-in nurses and visit them regularly? You should think seriously about their welfare and treat them well in their twilight years.

Investment options/regular reviews

All of the above questions are not easy to deal with. Everything eventually boils down to how much money you have. How much can you afford to put aside to meet all these beautifully laid-out plans?

Regular savings from your income are extremely important. You therefore need to pull your resources together, estimate reasonably your regular expenses and commitments without resorting to extravagance or a Spartan lifestyle, and save any balance in an interest-yielding account. Alternatively, the surplus could be split between savings and premium payments on life-insurance policies in the category that suits your circumstances. Life policies are important for both partners, to take care of any contingency such as a crippling illness, an accident, or even death. This is a contingency that must be taken care of, even if this means reducing current consumption. No one, with or without children, wants to start life afresh after a major disaster without anything to hang on to such as an insurance policy, savings, or other investments.

Many of these investments—land, houses, shares, stock options, profit-sharing plans including 401k plan in the USA, and insurance policies—can be sold or turned in during difficult periods or emergencies to take care of school fees or to facilitate relocating to another town. In making these decisions, try not to put all your eggs in one basket. Avoid being greedy by not putting your resources in mouthwatering investments. Diversify your investments in such a way that even if anything bad happens to some, others will be available to you to harvest. Recent corporate failures in 2001 and 2002 are an eye opener for all investors and workers who rely on their employers and growth in their share investments. The need for diversification can therefore not be overemphasized.

Remember that investments are built up over time in small portions. You can switch from one investment to another one that suits your plan better. What is more, there are always professional advisors to help you plan your investments— lawyers, accountants, estate agents, financial advisors, bankers, etc.—for a small affordable fee. Where necessary, if the proposed investment or cash outlay is large, you could ask for a second opinion, including a background check of the insurance company, bank, or estate developer you intend to use. Seeing a professional is advisable, at least to listen to what he has to say and then see if you agree with the advice given. Do not be afraid to ask questions or show your doubts, as it is your money you may be signing away.

Beware of making open-check payments directly to agents or advisors who could divert the funds to their personal accounts. Many unwary or unsuspecting investors have been duped in various ways, some even losing their entire life savings. So, be wary of mouth-watering proposals or promises. *Be smart and alert at all times.* Out there, there are people and organizations that are always on the lookout for the right people to dupe. At first, they look soft and well-mannered and pretend to have your interest at heart. Once they build up confidence and trust, they convince you to surrender all your money and investments and may disappear thereafter, to your eternal regret. Such stories abound in many countries.

There may be problems along your way in trying to realize the above plans. Of course, there will always be problems. This is natural. So, do not be disheartened, but continue making progress, falling and rising, but always rising up after each fall, until you realize your plans.

Whatever happens, your plans have to be reviewed regularly, say once in two or three years, to ensure that they are on course. If they are not, they should be changed to achieve more positive results. Even if they are on course, they should be updated or brought in line with contemporary realities because changes occur around us regularly.

Giving back to society

Lastly, remember to give back to society what you got from it. In this connection, belonging to charitable institutions to help the deprived, the sick, the disabled, and the less privileged members of society will be appropriate.

Active participation is necessary through giving your free time, money, and other resources, to assist the downtrodden. Where time and resources permit, you could assist the citizenry by providing transportation, housing, schools, hospitals, water, etc., for them all.

A time comes in one's life when one realizes that pursuing too much money is not healthy and that one gets more satisfaction from helping the disadvantaged. This idea may be one of your old age plans, instead of rocking away in an old people's home with only the four walls of your room to look at. This could quicken old age and your demise.

So learn to plan early and stick to your plans, no matter their imperfections. The best plans in the world—military, economic, social, religious, academic, etc.— usually have elements of imperfection.

Highlights

Planning for the future is essential. Leave nothing to chance.

Work out future plans that suit your circumstances.

Stick to the plans while reviewing or adjusting them periodically as circumstances dictate.

Learn to live with imperfections. No one or plan is perfect.

Chapter 13
Coping With Difficult Situations in Marriage

"Marriage, like life, is not a bed of roses. There will always be problems. Thus, there will be occasional thorns or pitfalls to be taken care of, confronted or avoided, rather than running away from them."

Imperfections of human beings

Human beings are no angels. Any person seeking 100 percent perfection in human actions may as well wait all eternity, or until all cows go to bed. Since no human being is born perfect, all of us must then learn to live with this imperfection. We should, therefore, make adjustments here and there so that life can go on. In short, *all imperfections should be recognized and understood.* In this connection, an attempt should be made to help those around, particularly spouses, children, the handicapped, and the less privileged members of society. Helping others facilitates accommodating them and adjusting our actions while limiting criticisms as well.

One basic thing a couple should learn early in their relationship is to trust and respect each other. Without this basic trust, you will live like a cat and a mouse and quarrel at the least provocation. Quarrels (not physical engagement) may be normal, but they should not go to the foundations of a marriage, e.g., faithfulness, active sex life, having children, accepting responsibilities, compromises, honesty, and love. Minor quarrels or misunderstandings not exceeding five to ten minutes can sometimes blow up into major quarrels, leading to serious distrust and eventual separation or even divorce. It is not the differences between couples that cause problems, but the way they are handled.

A low point in your life usually occurs when you quarrel with a loved one. The whole world seems to collapse around you. Sometimes, you do not even know what to do. This need not be so, as quarrels are normal. In the process, one learns what hurts the other party and tries to avoid sore areas in future dealings. People come out of quarrels stronger and learn to love and listen better.

Listening to your partner is very important. That is why a person who has been offended should approach the partner for explanations, in a very understanding and genteel manner. Many couples settle their differences internally and only invite outside help when they do not shift from their original positions or are unwilling to make compromises.

This step normally helps to ease tension and restore trust before an aggrieved party reaches wrong conclusions about what has happened. Where explanations given are apparently unsatisfactory or there are gaps, the aggrieved party should point them out in a nice manner. Sometimes it may not be necessary to pursue the matter any further, lest more unpleasant developments follow. A simple apology, whether or not from the heart (but it should be from the heart), helps a lot to soothe tempers. But how many couples realize this?

Instead of an apology, a man usually finds excuses for most of his actions and a woman quickly accepts them with equanimity, mainly to avoid rocking the boat. But when she is highly offended, the highest thing she can possibly do is refuse her husband's sexual advances for a couple of days until her anger, perhaps caused by the husband's flirtation, subsides. Then, normal activities resume.

On the other hand, when a wife offends her husband, she almost goes down on her knees to apologize. Yet, the husband takes his time to accept the apology and threatens "fire and brimstone," just to scare his wife stiff and bring her into total submission. The wife, in order to settle issues quickly, easily accepts whatever he says. In some African countries, such apologies from wives may come with fines imposed by the families of their husbands. These fines could range from a small amount of money or "drinks" to chickens or goats or a good combination of these. This merely goes to serve as a disciplinary measure and to emphasize the need for wives to respect their husbands and their marriages, as well as their in-laws.

This is just another way men have used over thousands of years to discipline their wives and bring them into total submission.

If couples are honest with themselves and have respect for the feelings of one another, ugly situations will hardly arise or last a long time. Little changes in one's behavior can sometimes go a long way toward changing the behavior of one's spouse.

Problem areas
However, in the course of living together, problems do arise, such as the following, among others:

Ill health
Flirtation/unfaithfulness/infidelity
Staying out late alone
Death of a partner, a relation, or an in-law
Performance of domestic chores

Settling or paying bills
Loss of a job or going to a job or laziness
Childlessness
Drunkenness and/or drug use and abuse
Children's welfare—school, health, safety, and care.
Inadequate sex life and/or loss of shape
Dirty habits in various forms
Interference by in-laws or friends
Abusive partner such as a man beating up his wife or children while under the
 influence, or if he is hot-tempered
Use of joint properties such as a car and/or a bank account
Sale of joint properties such as a house and/or a car

Problems are meant to be solved, one way or another.

Despite any problems that may confront partners in their marriage, they should never contemplate separation or divorce. This can never solve any problems. In fact, it may even worsen or compound their lives if children are involved. Perhaps, only in a very abusive or life threatening situation can separation be thought of, as a temporary measure, until normalcy is restored. Some couples have been known to live apart in the same country or city, but they still loved each other and visited one another regularly. In such circumstances, these couples feel that living together under the same roof causes quarrels and tensions, but they need to remain husbands and wives by living apart. They may be sexually active as husbands and wives or choose to remain without sex while they are living apart. This arrangement sounds rather strange, but not stranger than fiction. All the same, it has its merits. The marriages remain intact even though the partners live apart. The children stay with one of the parents but see the other parent once in a while. The two parents thus have controlling influence over the children. Contrast this with some situations where some parents "disappear" for many years, if not forever. So, living apart this way serves as a necessary compromise between outright divorce and living together under the same roof. It may not be the ideal thing to do, but it has its merits, as couples involved may some day come together again under the same roof.

Divorce can never be an answer to a marital problem. As was said earlier, it tends to complicate matters more. Partners get divorced to escape or avoid a loveless relationship and perhaps have the opportunity to look for a more interesting or fruitful relationship. Every action in life, including divorce, has a price. The price is often higher than anticipated and this inevitably leads to further frustration. Thus, dreams of happiness or heavenly bliss with a new partner may not materialize. This frustration may yet lead to another divorce or estrangement. Before you know it, you may be involved with so many divorces in your short life span of seventy five years or thereabouts.

How many in-laws do you want to have? Can you really remember the names of former spouses and children with each spouse, let alone their birthdays and other personal details?

Abuse of marriage vows/divorce practices worldwide

Some societies and even religions make divorce so easy that people are always willing to take advantage of this ease at the least provocation, as if their partners are to be discarded like old clothes. Some religions (including their ministers, some of whom are divorced) see marriage as an ordinary contract that can be broken with ease according to one's mood. Others, particularly Roman Catholics, see marriage as a sacrament that is indissoluble in the eyes of God and society.

Some civil courts, some Christians, some Moslems and some other religious practitioners, etc., ridicule this idea of marriage by using the same or similar oath "till death do us part" several times, even for professional divorcees. These groups accept the concept of divorce and are ready to wed those who have previously divorced. In these situations, the marriage vows should then be appropriately reframed to include words such as "till we decide to divorce or go our separate ways again and again or decide to come together as many times as we may want" rather than "till death do us part." This appears to make more sense to observers who expect about one third of marriages to end in the divorce courts, some even ending before the honeymoon is over.

While some societies and religions of all shades of opinions make divorce easy, others make it extremely difficult, thus giving parties the opportunity to change their minds and stay together continuously. Thus, under Islamic law with some conditions, a husband can divorce his wife by saying: "I divorce thee," three times, and by abstaining from sex with her for three months. The right words actually are "Talaq, Talaq, Talaq," which means divorce in Arabic. In some countries such as India where there is a significant Moslem following, some groups such as "Nisha" or "Women" are fighting the Moslem law of divorce by urging the federal government to register all Islamic marriages in civil courts rather than in Moslem clerics' registers. They are also requesting the government to ban the custom of allowing men to divorce their wives by simply saying "Talaq" three times. If such protests gain a large following, Moslem men may think of better and more decent ways to handle divorce. This appears to be necessary owing to women's emancipation and the need to give them the respect they truly deserve. There are slight variations here and there in the Moslem world.

This pronouncement, of course, can be revoked when the husband resumes sexual intercourse with his wife during the three months or withdraws the divorcing words. The problem here is that there may be no witnesses to the resumption of sexual intercourse or withdrawal of the divorcing words, if the husband denies and still wants to throw out his wife. It is the husband's word against his ex-wife's. Here, the husband has an advantage if he does not want his wife back.

In some Nigerian cultures particularly in the countryside, divorce, even though not widespread, is easily achieved by a man showing his penis to his wife and letting the tip of his penis touch the ground while pronouncing appropriate words. This process is called *"ISO-UTU"* in some Igbo cultures of Nigeria.

Women, not to be outdone, have their own way of divorcing their husbands. They simply show their husbands their open buttocks in a backward bent posture

111

while pronouncing appropriate words. This process is called "*IKPO-IKE*" in some Igbo cultures.

When these processes take place, reconciliation between husband and wife is never usually contemplated. The parties go their separate ways for life. However, these ancient practices have been largely abandoned due to Christian and other influences.

Abuse of the freedom to divorce and problems with it

Another noteworthy aspect of divorce is that there seems to be a strong relationship or positive correlation (not yet statistically proven, though) between economic independence and divorce. Thus, if partners are financially independent, divorce is more likely to take place at some time in their lives. Each of such partners is likely to be less yielding on certain matters or principles and is usually ready to damn the consequences of separation. On the other hand, divorce rate is low where spouses are dependent on each other and must cooperate to make ends meet. Furthermore, those who go into marriage early (between eighteen and twenty five) are more likely to get divorced than those who are patient until they reach their late twenties or early thirties.

If you get divorced, what is the guarantee that your next partner will be better than the one you divorced? There is none. Many a time, the new partner is worse than the one divorced. Must you walk down the marriage aisle ten or more times before you are satisfied with the last partner?

Have both partners thought of the *stigma* attached to being divorced? Has the woman involved thought of name changes and the problems likely to be caused—from Mrs. A, B, C, to Mrs. J, K, L—which will confuse her friends, relations, coworkers, and even her children from various husbands? Has she thought of the confusing surnames her children will bear—children having the same mother but several fathers? Has she also thought of the prospects of some of her children following in her footsteps and being ridiculed by their mates? What of the high likelihood of picking up sexually transmitted diseases or having children with crippling diseases and abnormal behavior along the way, in her bid to have an angel of a husband? The implications of divorce and remarriage are many and grave and should be seriously weighed.

There are alternatives to divorce such as legal or temporary physical separation, with the prospect of reaching accommodation with your partner in future, in the interest of the children. If necessary, you should ask for help from various organizations and relations on both sides. All these sources should be explored to the fullest. You should not shut your heart against reaching compromises in such trying situations.

To emphasize the need for couples to stay together, here is the story of an Italian couple who could not divorce because of their Catholic and family backgrounds. The wife caught her husband red-handed with another woman on their matrimonial bed, of all places. She subsequently refused to talk to, or sleep with, him for over *thirty years*. She had been deeply shocked by her husband's action.

There was no communication with each other during this period nor did they sleep together, let alone have sex. All the same, both of them played their other roles at home satisfactorily. The wife carried her anger too far because she so trusted her husband that (in her wildest dreams) she never expected him to talk to another woman, let alone take her to bed and on their matrimonial bed at that. The husband was clearly wrong on all counts. In the end, however, because of their children, who intervened, they amicably resolved the matter.

They have since been talking to each other and doing "other things" they missed for thirty years. As an old couple, they are not going to find it easy to catch up and enjoy all the fun they missed for thirty years when they were younger and more vigorous. It is hoped they have the stamina for all that.

There are also other couples who live in the same house but refrain from talking to one another except it is absolutely necessary, say, if the house is on fire or one of them is in serious danger. They also do not eat together or do anything together. They just stay under the same roof in the interest of their children. To outsiders, nothing seems wrong with the relationship.

Modern couples should therefore learn a lesson from the above story and others and seek out ways to solve their problems instead of running to lawyers and the courts for divorce. Because many divorce lawyers benefit from the monetary side and sometimes become a part of the love triangle, they never attempt to reconcile couples on the verge of divorce. Instead, they spend a greater part of available time (along with their agents) searching all records for hidden assets in order to enhance their fees from large divorce settlements. Couples also spend a lot of time moving assets around or hiding them to escape the searchlight of divorce lawyers, like the proverbial bird that keeps flying to escape sharp shooters.

Divorce in some notable Western nations has been taken to greater heights and it is probably now a part of their culture, particularly among royalty, actors, actresses, politicians, football stars, athletes, and notable public figures. The least suspicion of infidelity (just suspicion!) usually triggers divorce proceedings. These eventually attract undeserved and mouth-watering settlements running into several million dollars or its equivalent. These settlements, unfortunately, encourage more divorces and immoral living, including living above reasonable means, with the poor around begging just for crumbs. People are no longer ashamed to introduce themselves as divorcees or single parents. Divorce is now an accepted way of life, or so it seems.

Unfortunately, many countries have made divorce quite easy and rewarding. Even murder victims' families and other victims of rape, cruelty, and crippling accidents never usually get a fraction of what divorcees get in final settlement. Divorcees even sometimes ask for more after some years, basing their requests on previously omitted or new sources of income/assets of their ex-partners. With this kind of encouragement, there are now so many single parents (mothers and fathers, but mothers in particular) all over the place that it is tempting or appears fashionable to be one of them. But pains of single parenthood, loneliness, and the pressure to keep up are behind this "fashion" (or facade) of respectability.

Bringing up children to be law-abiding citizens has become increasingly difficult under one parent. Most of this burden, unfortunately, is borne by women.

For a man planning to divorce his wife, what are the implications? Must he, after apparently going through so many women before his marriage, marry up to ten wives before finally finding his "true love?" Must he throw women away as he does rags, including those that helped to build him up when life was rough? Has he forgotten that women or rather good wives are gifts from God? Has he suddenly realized that his wife is not as beautiful as his latest "catch," forgetting that this latest beauty will soon fade away like others before her?

If women changed partners half as frequently as men, the world would be an intolerable place to live in. Women tolerate men's actions a lot and are ready to make compromises much more easily than men. Yet, men do not seem to appreciate this and continue to humiliate women. Did you marry for beauty or shape, knowing that beauty is in the eyes of the beholder and may soon fade away? Where is the guarantee that the newest beauty will be better than the one divorced? In fact, if anything, the newest catch may be worse in all respects, judging from evidence of remarried men. What of children's welfare and their future behavior—like father like son? How many in-laws does a man wish to have? Is regularly changing wives all a man has to do? What of alimony payments being made? Are there no alternative uses to which these funds can be put?

Surely, many avenues are available for settling domestic disputes, but divorce is not one of them. In a divorce, all lose—the man, the woman, children, friends, relations and society. There are no winners.

Women are easy to "bend" like a twig if men treat them well. Men are also easy to handle if women respect and treat them well. Both men and women ought to realize early that separation or divorce hurts badly. To prove this, let each of them try picking up a quarrel with a neighbor or classmate or office colleague and not talk to each other for a month. They soon experience how it hurts. If this is so, how would you feel if your partner with whom you shared everything and who knew your secrets was involved? You are bound to have anxious moments at work and on the road. You will continue to make mistakes at work, at home, and on the road and take it out on those around you because of the frustrating developments at home.

Suggested solutions to problems

To avoid all of the above, a few helpful hints will be given in finding solutions to some possible problem areas mentioned earlier.

One major solution people usually ignore or forget when they have problems is prayers and voicing out their anxieties. People may sneer at this suggestion, but prayers do work, even if not immediately. They help to calm the nerves, are reassuring, and make people more confident about handling any problems. By praying, you are requesting that God, His angels, and saints intervene by presenting solutions to your problems. If you do not calm your nerves and the devil takes the better part of you, the consequences could be disastrous. You could be in hell fire in a matter of seconds if you do not allow good counsel to prevail. God knows the daily needs of people and He gives them what He approves, not necessarily what they ask for or expect. If God gave everyone what he or she requested in prayers, then the world would be impossible to live in because of conflicts of interests among humans. Hence God does the balancing act and gives to each person what is appropriate to his or her requirements, in their special circumstances, without hurting another party's interests.

Speaking from your heart to close friends or relations helps a lot to ease tension. Letting out what is bothering you may invite solutions from your listeners. In this way, the problem has probably been half-solved. You should not bottle up your problems or emotions. If you do not discuss them, people will naturally assume that all is well with you. If you do not speak out when you have a serious problem, you may become tensed up and in no time you may be battling high blood pressure, depression, and other serious ailments. Women tend to speak out more than men and this probably helps them live slightly longer than men, on the average.

Since patience is a virtue at all times, a man or woman having serious problems within a relationship should sleep over the problems and delay negative or provocative actions or saying anything that may be injurious to the relationship. Any angry words spoken or foolish actions taken are usually difficult to withdraw, as everyone tends to defend the position already taken. In fact, *silence* is effective and golden. Let it work positively for you. Louder than words, it speaks volumes and is pregnant with meaning. It gives you the opportunity to think of various courses of action to take when you are presented with problems.

Possible problem areas and solutions are:

1. Ill-health:

Being sick is no misfortune of any person or group. Anybody can fall sick at any time. What is important is the love shown and the help given to the sick and the disabled among us, particularly a spouse or a child.

Caring for the sick includes obtaining the best medical attention within available resources, providing food, helping to clean up any mess, saying soothing words, and keeping him/her clean, <u>inter alia</u>. Holding the hands of a sick person shows or signifies a lot of love. Where possible, a partner could cuddle the sick spouse and try romantic moves, and even go to the limits permissible and comfortable under prevailing circumstances.

Even if a partner is terminally ill, the best available treatment within the resources of the family should be provided to prolong the life of the sick person. This is the time for the strong and healthy partner to show love and compassion and to give assurance that both of them have had a wonderful time together and that, come what may, the sick partner's life and contributions will be cherished and remembered. This is not the time to abandon one's partner or to seek divorce simply because of this burden. You should now be the nurse, doctor, and comforter of the partner who is ill. If circumstances and prevailing mood permit, you could stretch your love further by performing any permissible acts, perhaps the very last ones, just to show your love. Above all, you should remember your wedding vows, particularly the part which states: "*in sickness and in health.*" You are expected to follow the spirit of those vows and look after your sick spouse.

2. Flirtation/Unfaithfulness:

Simply defined, adultery or unfaithfulness means sexual relationship between a legally married person and another person outside a legally recognized marriage. Lawyers and some other people may not agree with this definition, but at least the description of the act is obvious. Even at that, this subject is sometimes difficult to define in some cultures. This is so because *what is adulterous in one culture may be normal or routine in another culture*; so couples should define their own way of life and set out what activities or actions should be regarded as adulterous or tending toward it, particularly for couples who come from different cultural backgrounds. Some cultures limit adultery to married women only and see nothing wrong in the actions of married men who have multiple sexual relationships outside marriage. Ironically, some women support men in this regard. Their argument seems to be that only one woman for a man makes life boring and may always produce tension. By way of joke, too, there is a local saying somewhere in Nigeria that a man who sticks only to one woman risks losing his sex life and his libido. The actual saying in the native language is quite hilarious and raw, to the point.

Men, from time immemorial, have always been concerned about their wives' fidelity and have gone to great lengths to ensure this. In this regard, men have always felt that their wives belonged to them and could control or regulate their actions, while they, the men, were free to roam the entire world in search of sexual or other pleasures. Perhaps, this attitude on the part of men is *genetic*. This behavior is also found in the animal kingdom. Future research may come up with more explanations for men's behavior. Perhaps the already known hormone called testosterone may be blamed for this.

Thus, in some ancient cultures, some men required their wives to wear "chastity belts," which were padlocked. These were worn in such a way that men could not penetrate women except the belts were removed by the holders of the keys, in this case the husbands. Fortunately or unfortunately, this served a limited purpose, as some wives were known to make arrangements with blacksmiths for duplicate keys, to enable them sleep or have sex with their illicit lovers.

There were other instances when husbands put charms or voodoo (with so many variants) on their wives to enable the husbands catch their erring wives in the act. Thus, men's preoccupation with the faithfulness of their wives has not abated one bit to this day. Some men even go to the extent of hiring private detectives to shadow their wives secretly and report any acts of infidelity, real or imagined.

However, in various parts of the world, people usually engage in authorized or recognized sexual liaisons that are regarded as adulterous or abominable in other parts of the world. A few examples will be given:

a) A typical *Eskimo* usually offers his wife's sexual services to business partners and strangers visiting him. This is seen as a way of cementing relationships within business circles and the kindred. So, if a man abhors adultery or wife swapping, he should not visit an Eskimo with his wife or loved one; otherwise he may find himself and his Eskimo host exchanging partners. Perhaps visiting an Eskimo with your sister or someone other than your wife may be worth trying by those who are adventurous and want to find out the truth! It is hoped that you will like the Eskimo's wife.

b) Elsewhere, some primitive tribes, such as the Kofyar of Northern Nigeria, tolerate the keeping of partners or lovers within homes of married couples, if the latter find that their spouses are "sexually inadequate." The live-in lovers are supposed to makeup for this sexual inadequacy by having sexual liaisons under the same roof with the complaining spouses—perhaps, with the "sexually inadequate" partners listening in, watching, or simply seething in anger silently in a corner of the house. For some of the spouses watching, listening, or observing, this may be humiliating, but it is an accepted way of life. Other watching spouses may see some fun in it and even learn some valuable lessons about sexual encounters and positions. Older couples may need to learn all about foreplay which, apparently, was never a part of lovemaking by our ancestors. They rather went straight to the main point.

Even in many parts of Japan, China, India, Latin America, the Middle East, and Africa, adultery is a term usually applied to women only, provided the men do not go after sacred cows such as married women and innocent young girls. Once this simple "no-go area" rule is observed, anything goes for the men who, expectedly, exploit the situation. In such societies, sexual indiscretions or liaisons with forbidden groups could attract the death penalty (by stoning and other forms in some parts of the Moslem world) or chopping off the penis, for the offending men.

There is apparently no culture in which adultery does not exist, in one form or another. Despite the cruel punishment and stigma attached to it and the fact that there are even more tolerable and better alternative sexual liaisons available, people still continue to commit adultery. You should pause and think of the punishments, among others, meted out to offenders in some countries:

Public confession, along with heavy fines and performance of some humiliating acts in the full glare of everyone (in some African countries), like going "under the yoke" in Roman Empire times
Imprisonment
Divorce
Desertion/banishment
Death by stoning (in countries/areas having Moslem Sharia Law in place)
Burning
Choking
Ostracization

Public beating (also in some Moslem areas/countries).

Why should any person in his/her rightful mind try to commit adultery in any of these countries, in the face of these possible punishments? Yet, people see nothing wrong with it, as long as their sexual urge is satisfied, even if momentarily. Why is this so? Is it sexual variety, love for money or property, the urge to have better genes and thus healthier offspring, the need for some insurance or assurance of assistance in case of a partner's death, particularly a husband? Or is it the need to move with someone who is powerful or influential or the need to move up the corporate ladder? The answer may never be known as each person has his or her reasons for flirting or being adulterous. Thus, there are as many reasons as there are adulterers.

Adultery these days may prove more difficult to define and be accepted as having occurred. Take a good look at these scenarios and the moral and/or legal implications:

a) A man donates his sperm (not through sexual intercourse) to a childless married woman because of the low sperm count of her husband. Assuming she becomes pregnant and has a child, whose child is it—the sperm donor's or her husband's? Some may say that since she is still married, the child rightly belongs to her husband. Others may hold a contrary view that the child belongs to the sperm donor, who is regarded as the biological father. In some cultures, if a married woman flirts and has children while still legally married (even if she is separated from her husband), the children belong to her husband to whose name they must answer. But there are variations of this customary practice from place to place. Coming back to the question above, can it rightly be said that adultery has been committed, with or without her husband's consent, actual or implied? Ethics, religion, traditional practices, and the law probably have to be brought into all of this to be able to reach an acceptable solution or compromise and provide necessary guidance for the future. Thus, modern assisted conception techniques or practices still have so many moral, ethical, and legal questions to answer. Should all-embracing laws be passed to cover all possible outcomes? Should agreements be drawn and signed by all parties to cover these areas to avoid problems in future? Should all these arrangements be discreetly handled as is done in some cultures? Time will tell.

b) A husband is unable (for various reasons) to impregnate his wife and invites his close friend or relation to do the "job" for him, with the wife's full knowledge and consent. Did the friend or relation commit adultery if there was sexual liaison between them? Whose children would they be if children resulted from the liaison eventually? The same questions and ethical matters posed above seem to apply here. In some traditional setups, the children from such a liaison rightly belong to the husband. The wife, a key player in this liaison, and others who know about it are duty-bound, under pain of severe punishment, to keep quiet about it, so that the husband is not made the object of ridicule. In some cases, relations of the impotent husband even "nominate" a man for the wife, but the husband does not get to know him, obviously to protect the "nominee" from being attacked by a dangerous, jealous, and frustrated husband. Usually, when the wife is going to keep an appointment or date with her "nominated lover," she simply tells her husband that she is going to the market/mall or to some other place such as a hairdresser's. Her husband fully understands and dare not question her. She too, on her part, accepts this liaison for various reasons such as having her own children, being married into a wealthy family, and having all the respect and material benefits attached to it.

c) The third instance is where two men or even many more decide to marry one woman at the same time or at some point in time after the first husband has lived with his wife for quite some time. In some cultures, a man may find that it is extremely burdensome to maintain his wife. He then invites a brother or a friend to share his wife with him as an equal or co-husband. This arrangement looks far fetched but is quite common in very poor and populous countries. How and when they share the only wife is up to the men. In this instance, which of the men has committed or is committing adultery? Who is free from blame?

Some other marriage arrangements are full of odds and have the trappings of adultery as defined by some Christians and some legal systems.

A lonely and randy male traveler asks a hotel staff or someone else to introduce a lady to him for his "evening relaxation." The contact brings his wife or another married woman to the unsuspecting traveller in transit and collects his fees (whatever they are) for the introduction job. Later on, the traveler has a "good time" with the lady, not knowing that she is married. Has he committed adultery?

Sometimes women are used to entrap men who may be forced to pay a heavy monetary penalty before they are free to go. To avoid any problems or accusations, it is always good to check out the background of "introductions" or, better still, avoid any sexual liaisons with unknown persons in an unknown environment for the sake of your health and safety. One therefore needs to ask if someone is married or not, as one may not wish to rock a marriage boat or even be accused of rape or sexual indiscretion.

Still talking about adultery, many men and, regrettably, an increasing number of women, engage in extramarital affairs these days, in a brazen manner, even in the full glare of their aggrieved partners. Men generally (and genetically!) tend to be less forgiving than women when their spouses are caught in the act. It is usually always devastating and humiliating for a man to know that his wife is flirting or sleeping around with other men. It is even more hurtful if she is caught red-handed. Nothing injures a man's ego faster. The "man" in him disappears quickly. Professional and economically independent or strong women tend to engage in extramarital affairs more than their traditional counterparts or other groups.

Women, on the other hand, perhaps because of their genetic makeup and other assumed disadvantages, tend to be very forgiving, so long as their husbands keep illicit relationships as casual as possible and also take care of them materially and sexually. Men thus appear to be far guiltier of adultery or unfaithfulness for various reasons rooted in their sex genes, culture, economic strength, the natural tendency for men to be polygamous, and the natural tendency for some women to fall for the lies, sweet-coated words, and promises of men. Why should a decent woman, for instance, encourage a man to divorce his wife and marry her instead? Women should understand that men who tell them they no longer love their wives are not to be taken seriously. If they listen to their deceit, they have themselves to blame. On the other hand, if a man tells a woman that he is well married and living with his wife, this is the guy who should be listened to, as he is neither afraid to tell the truth, nor is he willing to deceive a woman for a momentary enjoyment.

As one cynic observed, there has been only one major instance when a woman successfully deceived a man—Eve versus Adam in the biblical Garden of Eden. Since then, men have taken over. They deceive women and tell lies in various forms in order to take them to bed, which is the highest ambition of any man going after a woman. Thus, the cynic further observed: "Any man who tells a woman the truth never succeeds in 'conquering' her or bringing her under control." How true! But please tell the truth as much as possible, especially if it affects a person's well being and happiness. No black lies! Perhaps, some little white lies on the humorous side!

Women have thus tended to be the victims of the waywardness of men. If your spouse is a confirmed flirt, you should have observed this during courtship, or perhaps it escaped your detection. People flirt for various reasons, ranging from unsatisfactory sex in a relationship to the need for revenge, cash, or other favors. Other reasons include the need to be seen among the opposite sex, the need to get over loneliness or problems, the need to have a taste of it or have some experience to talk about. For every flirt on the face of the earth, there is a genuine reason and even a unique reason for flirting.

It may even sound quite paradoxical to say that the more a person flirts or has affairs, the more that person loves the partner being cheated. This is so because human beings tend not to appreciate what they have (good wife/husband/friends/parents) until they are on the verge of losing them or are in a big fix or mess. It may sound even more paradoxical to say that if a man does not look at or admire gorgeous women, he will not admire or look at his wife. Men are supposed to admire women, particularly those who are flashy, beautiful, or influential. So, the mere fact that a husband looks at, or admires, other women does not mean he has ceased to love his wife. Wives should not blow their tops when they catch their husbands looking at women on the streets or in magazines or television. They are only committing what people, particularly humorous ones, loosely call "the sin of lookery"—just looking and admiring them without going any further. Women should also understand that most men, if not all, do not attach emotions to sex, unlike women. If therefore a woman catches her husband "fooling" with another woman, she should weigh all circumstances and explanations before taking any drastic or foolish action, if at all. It does not mean that he is planning to leave her or is tired of her or does not enjoy her lovemaking. He is just being animalistic and showing his machismo or libido. Animals in the jungle do the same thing. Some animal species are even worse, as they perform sexual acts right before on-looking or other sexual partners in their harem or territory and even before their offspring. Human beings are probably the only "animals" who hide when having sex with loved ones, of course discounting live sex shows that are meant to entertain patrons.

These suggestions or views do not, in any way, support the foolish actions of some men. They are not meant to encourage licentiousness on their part. All illicit actions of men and women in this love game have their cost or price, which must be paid sooner or later.

Whatever reasons are given, there are no acceptable excuses for flirting, which is probably as old as humanity, or at least dates back to the time when people began living together in groups. There are serious dangers in flirting including losing one's partner, rage and jealousy that could lead to murder, letting children copy this behavior, passing STDs to innocent spouses and future generations and causing breakup of families. For a woman in particular, there are social stigmas associated with flirting. In nearly all societies, it is taboo for a married woman to flirt or commit adultery. Where this occurs in some societies and she wants to get reconciled with her husband, some "cleansing" has to be done on her, supposedly to ward off evil forces that could destroy her family. In such societies, a woman's body is considered "sacred." Men who have affairs with married women in such societies are also disciplined and where a relation's wife is involved, the punishment is quite severe and humiliating, as a warning to other men.

The underlying reasons for flirting should be sought. Couples should talk this over and settle the matter with promises not to go astray again. It takes a large heart to forgive a spouse who has gone astray. Forgiving an erring and apologetic spouse is probably better and easier than starting a new relationship or having a divorce. Remember that to err is human, but to forgive is divine. No partner should take the other for granted, particularly the man who tends to flaunt his affairs for his wife to see and apparently dare her to do whatever she wants. Men should remember that a woman has a far greater capacity to destroy her husband than the husband has. When she discovers that her husband is cheating on her quite openly, she feels used and betrayed and is ready to destroy him. A woman does not easily forget matters that involve sex because all her emotions are tied to her sexuality. Her whole life is tied to it. If she truly loves, she does so with her whole heart, with a lot of passion. Her milk of human kindness and her motherly love quickly manifest themselves. But if she hates, she equally does so with passion and the "devil" in her quickly manifests itself. Thus, if she does not like a man and has an opportunity to destroy him, she can even raise charges of rape or assault against him. However, if a man is a "devil" but loves her, she will remain with him and may, with passion, even help him achieve his evil designs. You should watch some police reports on male criminals and their wives or girlfriends and see how the latter help their partners commit crimes or cover them up.

Separation or divorce, as has been said before, does not solve any problem. Would any one like to lose his or her partner to a rival who might even be inferior in many respects? People should stay within their marriage and solve any problems rather than start a new love relationship that may prove to be a failure even before it begins, or worse than the earlier failed relationship. So, men and women have to be extremely careful and keep promises made, or not make any promises at all, including actions that imply a tacit or actual acceptance of any suggestions or agreements.

In connection with some men's flirtatious behavior, some wives have tried to deal with the serious matter and accommodate it by doing a number of things, thus avoiding separation or divorce, particularly where such women did not want to start new relationships. They would rather deal with the "devils" already known than handling "angels" who might turn out to be worse in future; so take a close look at these actual stories and learn some valuable lessons in handling flirts. Patience and humor may be all it takes:

Case # 1.

The wife of a traveling executive officer who had roving eyes for women always made sure her husband took along a pack of condoms. She put it in his suitcase herself and urged him to always use them if he needed to. At least this was one bold way of ensuring that her husband protected himself from STDs. Through this way, she too would never have STDs from her husband. How wise! Her efforts paid off gradually as her husband stopped flirting and took her on tours sometimes. It has been a very successful marriage. What a sensible wife!

Case # 2.

Another young wife had a funny but ingenious way of "disarming" her husband when he was going out alone. She would jokingly ask him to ensure that he talked only to ladies who were far more beautiful than she was. Of course, the ladies' man always behaved when he went out alone and never flirted. He would even joke back on his return and say that he searched and searched for a very pretty lady but found none.

Case # 3.

Still another tactic used by another housewife was most practical and beneficial to the couple. She would have great sex with her husband before he went out alone, thus effectively weakening him and taking his mind and eyes away from beautiful ladies he might see outside. Women have known from time immemorial that a great number of men, if not all, do not easily have an erection until many hours have elapsed after the first one.

So wives having husbands with roving eyes should look for ingenious ways to ensure they do not stray for long, if at all. They should always make room in their hearts for forgiveness, understanding, and reconciliation. This is far better than separation or divorce, all things being equal.

3. Death Of A Partner:

This is the most hurtful aspect of a relationship, particularly if the couple lived together and loved each other so much. It is a burden that has to be borne throughout the life of the surviving partner. Couples who have been so close have sometimes been found unable to cope when one of them died. The survivor usually followed or died in a matter of months or a few years, being unable to live alone. A departed partner should be given a befitting burial, taking into account available financial resources, customary practices, religious practices, and the deceased's expressed wishes, if any, when he or she was alive.

The surviving partner should assume all responsibilities, in the interest of the children who may still be young. Help from all available quarters will be needed and should be explored. If one does not make the request, it may not be given, in the mistaken belief that one does not need help. The survivor should think positively about life and the future of the children and family members, be close to in-laws and friends who remain friendly, obtain insurance and other benefits if available and invest the proceeds wisely. It is when tragedies such as death occur that one remembers the importance of having a planned life and then knows true friends and relations. The departed partner should be remembered in prayers regularly and on the anniversary of the death.

The surviving partner should not rush to have another partner if he or she does not actually need one, particularly if there are grown up or adult children in the previous relationship. Obviously, company is needed, as mourning cannot go on forever. Furthermore, the widow or widower has a life to live and should continue from where both of them left off. Any new relationship should be well defined, as children may not be quite receptive to the idea of having a stepfather or a stepmother. So as much as possible, the idea of having another spouse should be sold to the children gradually. In this way, their minds will be well prepared for the day the final decision is made to have another spouse.

However, where children are not involved, i.e., if the relationship did not produce any children and one has the inclination to have some, then one should do what is proper. Courtship has to be started all over again, as if one were a beginner in the love game. Do not be surprised if you find yourself behaving like a young person in love: calling your companion many times a day, saying "sweet nothings" over the telephone, visiting and expressing your undying love, observing your companion, among other courtship behaviors. You should never try to compare your new partner or companion with the departed one because no two human beings have the same personality, even if they are from the same parents.

4. Domestic Chores:

Depending on customary practices, some domestic chores are specifically meant for the man or woman, but not both, except if they are living apart. There are really no ironclad rules about this usually problematic area. This should be understood by both partners, so that one does not start accusing the other of not helping enough, if at all. Generally, a man should perform very difficult and dangerous tasks while a woman performs softer or easier (even if more tedious) chores such as cooking, washing of dishes, washing up children, and cleaning the home. The man thus fixes broken-down appliances, washes and irons clothes, services cars, drives children to and from school, ensures reasonable security around the house, among other chores. When his wife is pregnant, he should show some understanding by helping her frequently at home, as there is no hard and fast rule about all this. Cooperation and understanding are the key words here. Where maid services can be afforded, they should be used. Gentle persuasion from the wife can get her husband to do a lot more than his fair share. But unnecessary bickering and shouting may get her nowhere. The husband can also use some flattery to get his wife to do more than her fair share of chores when necessary. Partners should remember that small quarrels often lead to serious ones, which could strain their relationship, so partners should watch their utterances carefully. If a partner has no soothing words to use in order to calm a charged atmosphere, it is better to remain quiet.

5. Drunkenness and Drug Abuse:

If a partner is usually drunk, or is judged to be on hard drugs (such as heroin, marijuana, metamphetamine, ecstasy, etc.), this can be devastating to the other partner. Either problem is capable of killing or wasting someone gradually; so, the problem should be addressed early.

In addition, drunkards and drug users can be out of their minds. This often leads to spousal and child abuse in various forms. It can also lead to death in the family if the habit continues without control or any form of rehabilitation. The sober partner should report the matter promptly to relations and friends who are in a position to help. If this approach fails, welfare units should be approached for help in rehabilitating the drunkard or drug user. There are institutions that specialize in this kind of rehabilitation; so, the affected spouse should be sent to one of them. Of course, the treatment is not free; so a way has to be found to foot the bill.

Regrettably, both sexes are now fully involved in this dreadful habit. In the past, it was unusual to find a drunkard or an ardent drug user among women. However, since their "liberation" from men, women have found "freedom" in the use of alcohol and hard drugs in order to be even with their male counterparts. To such women, men have apparently since been monopolizing this age-old field and should be checkmated. As regards this regressive habit, doctors have been warning pregnant women against the dangers of using alcohol and drugs. Their offspring could be adversely affected.

Under the above prevailing conditions, the "clean" person may find it difficult to continue living under the same roof with the partner for fear of being physically harmed. If this danger is real—having been actually experienced or it is a serious threat—the clean partner whose life is in danger should consider moving elsewhere temporarily until sanity returns. But if the partner being treated is not in any way violent, then there is no need for temporary separation. Of course, in all of this, there is no room for divorce. It is a lame excuse to cite this problem of drunkenness or drug abuse, as the sober partner is supposed to assist the drug user to come clean. It is a cross that has to be carried, even if it is for life.

6. Lack of a Job:

This should not be a problem except a partner is lazy. The working partner should assume all responsibilities in the meantime. Needless to say that all expenses must be reviewed and cut down or cut out as much as possible in order not to accumulate unpaid bills. Since both husband and wife are one, they should plan and work together always. If they have planned well, they can fall back on some savings to meet pressing bills that are in the nature of fixed expenses. These include, but are not limited to: rent, telephone charges, television/cable expenses, school fees, insurance, light, fixed bills, etc., which accrue periodically and must be paid. The nonworking partner should do a lot to help out at home and encourage the employed partner. All efforts should be made by the unemployed partner to secure a job as soon as possible or retrain for a new job, lest the working partner (if it is the wife) start to complain about taking on too much family burden. A man should see it as his primary responsibility to feed, clothe and protect his family. His wife is supposed to play only a supportive role, not a primary role. After all, the burden of pregnancy, childbirth, and child rearing or upbringing is more than enough for her to carry. Hasn't nature given her so many burdens already?

7. Non-arrival of Children:

Many couples face this problem and it is even worse for those who are perfectly healthy. Since only God gives children, a couple should not lose sight of this fact and should therefore continue praying. They should go for checkups to find out where the problems lie and what should be done to correct any problems or deficiencies in the entire reproductive systems of both partners. Children sometimes arrive late. All the same, a couple should continue loving each other as they had promised to do when they took their wedding vows. Where, however, a couple feels strongly about this issue, particularly for those advancing in age, they should consider adoption in the meantime and continue their efforts to have children of their own. Where they can afford it, modern methods should be tried as long as the ethics of it all and possible future controversies have been well explained, understood and taken care of by them. There can be no question of divorce or separation due to lack of children in the relationship. In some countries where this kind of problem cannot be put up with for long, some intending couples sometimes prefer to have children outside wedlock first before formally getting married. Where such sexual liaisons before marriage do not produce children, separation of partners is easier and less painful. However, this is not to be encouraged if the partners love themselves.

In an effort to have children, particularly those of a particular sex, some men resort to having several wives or partners. Having children of the same sex and other marital issues have usually compounded such men's problems. Apart from very primitive societies, the sex of a child is no longer a problem or of any importance to people throughout the world. Those who favor male sex will be shocked to know that it is usually female children who are more inclined to take care of their aged parents than male children. The latter usually have more than enough marital and other burdens or pleasures of their own to bear or enjoy and therefore won't pay much attention to the plight of their parents.

8. Abusive Partner:

Abusive partners are now very common and the number, regrettably, is growing, even among eminent and well-informed people and celebrities. Abusive partners, particularly men, tend to treat their "better halves" or "alter egos" as trash or inferior persons having no rights or feelings whatsoever, as if they are robots to be controlled at the touch of a button. Abuse takes various forms ranging from spousal beating, shouting unnecessarily at partners at the least provocation, emotionally abusing them, making lewd or obscene remarks about their persons, raping them, not providing reasonably for their welfare, to messing up the home after drinking and expecting partners to clean up the mess. Sometimes the abuse may involve locking up a spouse all day in a basement and not allowing him or her any access to telephone, food, friends, or relations. Maltreating children and not loving them enough are included. Like other problem areas, an abusive situation requires careful handling. Help should be sought through counseling and constant discussion. Fighting back occasionally helps. This is similar to fighting back an enemy when he pursues you to the wall. Since you have no other place to run to, you will fight with all your might as if it is your last battle. In time, the enemy is bound to get weak and retreat.

If an abused partner allows the spouse to continue abusing him or her, a sadist will surely enjoy the situation and continue, with little or no consequence. In some cases, the abused partner is afraid to seek help or even report to appropriate authorities. But if there is some fighting back, the abused partner may soon gain the much-desired respect and not be taken for granted again. Peace may then be given a chance.

In this connection, the story is told about a man who usually beat up his wife at the least provocation. Out of respect for her husband, she never fought back and the idiot of a husband took this as weakness or timidity on her part. Then one day, she summoned up courage and stood up against the abusive husband. She lifted him easily, floored him, and beat him up repeatedly. Out of shame, the husband never complained to anybody. He was really shocked, to say the least. Peace and respect, which eluded the couple for many years, were instantly restored to the home forever.

However, not all abused wives can be this lucky. It is even unthinkable for a man to physically and emotionally abuse his wife and expect her to respond to his sexual advances later at night. She is no longer emotionally attached to him. She will no longer enjoy any sexual relations with him, unless he changes his attitude and woos her back.

Increasingly too, regrettably, some women have begun to abuse their partners just as some men have done all along. When a woman appears to earn more money than her husband, has more "bluish" blood or is larger in frame, the possibility of abuse is always there. First, she tends to become unruly and challenges her husband's suggestions and even requests him boldly to do those chores normally reserved for women. When she goes out, she stays out as long as possible and does not offer any explanations even when asked, talk less of an apology.

Cases are not unknown of some strong wives who usually beat up their husbands, send them to the floor and sit on them. But when neighbors intervene, the wives quickly switch positions, placing their battered husbands on themselves and shedding crocodile tears, thus making it look like their husbands have been beating them. Of course, such men will never admit that their wives beat them up, as this is regarded as shameful and humiliating. After all, women are supposed to be the "weaker" sex in terms of brute strength. Furthermore, many husbands are usually *henpecked* or nagged into submission and total silence by unruly and shrewish wives. Such husbands are too scared to open their mouths while their wives rattle away.

Couples also abuse their children in various ways. Children are forced to perform dangerous chores that are not normally meant for them. They are not sent to school, are pushed to the streets to work and prostitute, are constantly harassed and not praised at all, are denied basic necessities, are not allowed to play or mix with their colleagues, are dangerously beaten and tortured, are not treated when they are sick, and are sometimes sexually abused while other welfare matters are compromised. Any person who discovers such abuses or suspects they exist should call appropriate authorities to investigate. Advice could also be given to abusive parents who may be quite ignorant of the consequences of their actions.

If only some parents knew the pains undergone by childless couples and expenses incurred by them in their bid to have children of their own, they would treat their God-given children as gold.

Abusive situations, however, are not an excuse for divorce or separation. Compromises can be worked out and couples can make it up to each other. The earlier abusive tendencies are discovered and checked, the better for all, before they lead to dire consequences such as death or debilitating injuries.

A number of situations can be considered abusive. Partners should therefore look out for these and others and take *appropriate actions.*

Here goes:

a. Use of foul language on a regular basis
b. Use of threat or force to obtain something or information including sex or to stop someone from saying or doing something freely
c. Actual use of a weapon such as a gun, knife, baseball bat, or even furniture on a spouse
d. Not allowing a spouse to explain a situation
e. Not allowing a spouse freedom to call friends or relations or to go out alone sometimes
f. Locking up a spouse at home or in a place where the spouse cannot call for help or move around
g. Actually beating up a spouse, spitting on the spouse, or performing other acts of humiliation including attempts to poison the spouse
h. Not helping a sick spouse to obtain medical services
i. Denying sexual pleasure to a spouse and not participating wholeheartedly
j. Not allowing a spouse to work or go to school or train for a job

k. Not allowing a spouse to practise the religion of choice
l. Not helping a spouse perform some domestic chores
m. Other abuses in varying degrees and forms.

As soon as a spouse observes any of these signs and it appears matters are getting worse or out of hand, the victim or intended victim should flee to safety, away from the abusive environment. This may lead to a temporary or permanent separation, depending on the extent of abuse and the readiness of the oppressor to change positively. Thus, the most important thing at this point in time is to be alive and be able tell the story later, perhaps in court.

While no spouse should tolerate a serious abuse for long, it is highly advisable that the victim avoid responding on the spot, or in a face-to-face situation by shouting back, as the abuser may react violently and terminate the life of the victim on the spot. The victim should do whatever is necessary to stay alive even if this means pledging false love to distract the abuser. The victim should not wait to be killed simply because he or she does not want outsiders to know what is happening. Remember that a living dog is better than a dead lion. Avoid any injury or harm to yourself. *After all, the first law of nature is self- preservation.*

Incidentally, children are also abused, so the above in varying degrees may apply to children. The victim and children should flee to safety at the most opportune time. Spouses, friends, and neighbors should be on the look out and assist those in need through advice and reporting to authorities.

9. Other Problems:

There are other problems that usually arise which should be sorted out at a couple's level. One thing a couple should always do is keep talking, advising, singing, laughing, watching out for changes in mood, and showing understanding and love. One day, the partner who has been causing troubles will see the need to change for the better. Marriage, from time immemorial, has never been known to be a bed of roses. It has been a mixture of roses and thorns. If one makes up one's mind and becomes bonded to a partner, one has no cause to complain. One simply has to bear or carry one's cross throughout life. If help comes your way, it is okay, but if not, do not begrudge anybody.

It is indeed surprising how some couples have ended their marriages simply because dinner was served late or that the wrong toothpaste was purchased or for other bizarre reasons. Where have people's patience and tolerance gone? Can people no longer control their tempers and shut up a little bit? Do the frustrations of modern living and accompanying stress contribute to problems being experienced by couples? Patience, sharing, and forgiveness seem to have become dead virtues. A little quarrel or misunderstanding may end up in shooting, while a little dent on a car or nonpayment of a little sum of money may invite court action or murder.

Everyone must work hard to reverse these unfortunate events or trends called divorce, separation, intolerance, unfaithfulness and abuses within relationships called marriages.

Again, it must be recognized that there usually cannot be two captains in a ship, to avoid conflicting instructions and to promote harmony among the crew and passengers. In the same way, within a home, the voice or authority of one of the partners must be seen to prevail. The voice is usually that of the husband, who should also exercise the greatest responsibility in using this authority. His wife is a copartner, even if a junior one, and has equal rights with him. But he is simply <u>primus inter pares</u>—first among equals. Accordingly, the wife should respect this authority as much as possible to ensure marital harmony and discipline within a home. Thus, the wife should always discuss with her husband all major issues concerning her, to sound out his views and obtain support if necessary. In this way, if anything goes wrong, her husband will easily come to her rescue and give needed support.

Things/Matters to avoid when you are under stress

Finally, it is good to remember always that when one is under pressure or stress from domestic or office problems, one should try to remove the pressure by relaxing and making up to one's partner in various ways. However, one should *avoid doing* the following things during this period:

Having sex, as there may be no urge or good erection for the man or any romantic feelings for both partners. The woman may even experience dryness all the way.

Taking *major decisions,* as one's thinking may not be at its best. One may regret any such decisions throughout life.

Driving for a long distance, if at all, as one may be absent-minded.

Studying or doing a write-up, as one's thoughts may be incoherent.

Taking it out on one's children, office colleagues, and neighbors, as they are innocent.

Saying something or accusing your partner of something you are not sure of or cannot prove.

Handling any dangerous weapons or tools, as they may be used wrongly or carelessly and may result in injury to, or death of, someone.

In short, you should have nothing to do with any thing that requires concentration. If you require additional proof or additional information, then obtain it and critically examine it before taking any decisions or rushing into any judgments.

With all of the above in mind, a pessimist may be inclined to lose faith in marriage and say it is too difficult a union to be in. But is there any aspect of life that is not difficult? Even eating, drinking, or having sex is difficult. Will you abandon living with your neighbors or even sharing planet earth with lower animals simply because they are difficult to deal with or that your neighbors' lifestyle does not rhyme with yours? This, as you know, will be selfish, as you are not an island to yourself.

Highlights

Trust and respect each other.

Deal with a problem with a positive attitude and nip it in the bud before it rattles a relationship.

Divorce or separation does not solve any problem; rather, it tends to compound it and your own life.

Remember that a man plays a primary role in the family while a woman plays a supportive or secondary role; however, this may be reversed in certain situations, which loving couples should understand and deal with.

Adultery or unfaithfulness should be avoided, as this is perhaps the greatest single factor that destroys a relationship, leading also to dire consequences.

All should learn to forgive and overlook some behaviors as many times as offenders repent. This approach promotes peace and rest of mind.

Ask for help from trusted third parties if problems cannot be settled internally. Do not bottle up any problems, as they are solvable.

Do not take certain decisions or handle dangerous objects when you are under pressure or stressed out.

Chapter 14
Mending Broken-Down Marriages

"Dealing with a 'devil' you know is easier and better than dealing with an 'angel' you do not know and whose behavior you cannot predict."

Consequences of separation/divorce

The figures are staggering. They have reached epidemic proportions in some countries. They include the old and the young, princes and princesses, the rich and the poor. They cut across cultural lines, races and religions, even among those that do not formally authorize divorce or separation. They include first, second, third, fourth, fifth, and sixth marriages and more. The figures keep rising yearly. Figures towards the end of the chapter should shock you as being astronomical for the various countries, particularly the dishonorable "leading candidates."

These may not be alarming to some people who do not believe in marriages, much less their indissolubility. However, to others who are inclined toward puritanism, the figures speak of fast, morally declining societies where children are not brought up under the influence and love of both parents. In many of these cases, spouses having custody of children always have something negative to say to the children about their ex-spouses, who no longer live with them. Children may be thus influenced to start hating or having negative attitude towards those spouses and the sex groups or genders to which the ex-spouses belong.

These are all broken-down marriages, in which spouses are already physically separated or divorced, or are still living under the same roof in name only and are in the process of becoming history as husbands and wives. The figures have more than doubled in the last twenty years. Thus, it is now relatively easy to project that out of so many marriages contracted in a year, about one third may end in separation or divorce within the first year. With almost one third of the married population either divorced or separated, the time is fast approaching, perhaps within twenty years, when a majority of marriages will end in total failure. As a consequence, there will be single parents who have children and a carefree way of life that may adversely affect the character of children under them. From this lifestyle, societies may graduate into no sex with partners, while computers and other machines mix sperm and eggs in a "magical womb" to produce children who will run the world in their own machine minded ways. Human beings are never to be trusted when it comes to experimenting for monetary benefits. This scenario is neither far away nor far fetched; so, you should not laugh. Science fiction, which we see in movies many a time, becomes reality in a short time. Sometimes, truth is stranger than fiction.

Artificial insemination in animals and humans, which has been practised for long, looks like child's play these days, as compared with various trials or experiments now going on in the science world. Thus, animal cloning, which scientists have been practising under cover until recently when some Scottish scientists admitted that they had successfully cloned a sheep (Dolly), may yet lead to human cloning in the years ahead. Some advocates of human cloning have even predicted that human parts (to replace diseased or aging parts of the body) will become easily available under supermarket conditions in the not-so-distant future, but at what cost? Imagine buying human parts in a supermarket! Such advocates have tried to make a distinction between *therapeutic cloning* (using stem cells from discarded human embryos for research purposes with a view to curing some diseases) and *reproductive cloning* (using stem cells to produce human clones).

This, to say the least, is pure semantics. Cloning is cloning, no matter the end result or use. Will such clones be regarded as human beings with equal rights and respect, which are accorded to those conceived naturally? A lot of legal and ethical issues still need to be sorted out. So far, a great majority of people, national governments, and virtually all major religions are strongly opposed to human cloning. The opposition is generally throughout the world. If societies were to succumb to the wishes of human cloning advocates, the world would soon witness a situation whereby some medical personnel might start to remove eggs from the ovaries of women without their consent. It might even lead to abduction and killing of women simply because people would like to harvest their eggs. This would eventually lead to a great black market for human eggs required for stem cell experimentation. Opposition to this process continues to be very strong around the world. This is the position today. Tomorrow is uncertain. Advocates and opponents of human cloning (in whatever form) still have a field day. The group which wins will continue to hammer home its views.

Will human life be degraded or enhanced through cloning? Time will tell.

It would have been thought that in some countries where costs of divorce and settlement are outrageously high—running into several millions of dollars or pounds sterling—couples would have begun to tolerate each other and never again talk of separation or divorce. But no! It does not matter whatever it costs to get rid of an unwanted or unloved partner. Money is easy to make from various entertainment sources and other areas of human endeavor. The advocates of divorce think that they have all eternity to live and fool around and that they are never going to be accountable for their actions. They are mistaken, for accountability is around the corner. It is usually when such people fall from "grace to grass" that they start to mend their ways in the mistaken belief that their excesses have been forgiven, without any form of restitution or reconciliation.

Even if you do not love your partner, why can't you pretend in the interest of peace, family harmony, and for God's sake? After all, there are many situations in life which people accept, even though they do not like them.

You may not like your nose, ears, legs, breasts, face, or stomach. But will you cut them off? Will you go to war because you do not like your neighbor for whatever reasons? You should remember that you took an oath to love, honor, preserve, and protect your partner until separated by death.

Many years ago, only a few reasons could be advanced for divorce, such as infidelity, infertility or impotence, wrong match, or desertion. These days every excuse and any reason under the sun could be advanced for divorce or separation. Divorce courts can hardly cope with numerous reasons being advanced today. Couples rush to divorce their spouses, even on false or trumped-up charges.

The most popular reason seems to be *"incompatibility of partners,"* which means anything (real or imagined) made up by the complainant, according to his or her mood.

What is the world turning into—a kind of circus where men and women play out themselves and outmaneuver one another as if marriage is no longer fashionable, as envisaged by God? Why are marriages breaking down so fast, some even before the ink on dotted lines has dried up, and even for couples who have been married for twenty or more years? Are men and women no longer committed? Do they no longer know what honor is? Do they want a society where there is no permanent attachment to men or women and where men and women are matched at random by the computer for sexual encounters only, which should last no longer than one hour? What then happens to women who become pregnant or to children born through this arrangement? Even under repressive or communist systems of government of various shades, this approach was never considered, let alone implemented. Under this untried and noncommittal arrangement, there will be nothing like love as people know it and around which human procreation depends. People will only have sexual relations and not "make love" with all their heart and emotions attached to lovemaking. Yet, love is the main driving force in nature, which makes living worthwhile, even among animals. You love someone and someone loves you in return. This applies to parents/children, husbands/wives, citizens/societies, and the larger world of various countries coming together to foster friendship, cooperation, and understanding in a number of ways.

Some people do not yet appreciate the impact of divorce on children who have been brought up under single parents or no parents at all. Children do not understand why their parents decide to live apart. Societies appear to be producing more criminals through delinquent and single parenting. Prisons are full and are costing nations a lot of resources to maintain them. Unless societies strengthen the bonds of marriage and make divorce relatively difficult, children and values as well as bonds of love handed down over several generations may be doomed.

Cost of marital breakdown on children

Children obviously seem to suffer most in a marital breakdown. This may not be obvious until later years, say, in their twenties and thirties. From research works around the world spanning so many decades, it has been reported, among other problems, that generally:

> Children in a home where there is no father usually suffer poverty, emotional heartache, ill health, lost opportunities, and instability.
>
> They are 50 percent more likely to suffer health problems, twice as likely to run away from home, and many times as likely to suffer various forms of abuse.
>
> They are three times as likely to experience difficulty getting on with other people and to struggle at school or at work.
>
> The same children, as teenagers, are almost twice as likely as their mates living with two parents, to drink, smoke, have underage sex, and even become teenage parents.

Even where married couples were as poor and underprivileged as single parents, their children were generally less likely to experience such problems.

Of course, there are exceptions here and there as in all rules. Thus, good children could come out of broken homes while bad children could graduate from homes of happily married couples.

However, the point has been made that children are generally better off when their parents stay together.

Because of the high divorce rate, it is the duty of all—state, religious bodies, friends, kinsmen, and relations—to bring down this rate significantly. People should not fold their hands and watch divorcing couples debase the marriage institution for their selfish ends.

Before going further, you may wish to go back to Chapter 13 dealing with difficult situations in marriage. The following paragraphs are an appropriate extension of that chapter.

Main causes of broken-down marriages

What are the *main causes* of broken-down marriages? These can be traced, but not limited, to:

1. Greed—One party tries to take advantage of the partner's fortunes, and literally "creates" conditions for divorce, to his or her delight.
2. Intolerance—One partner does not tolerate the spouse and imposes difficult wishes on the partner without trying to reach a compromise in the interest of both parties.

3. Short Courtship—A couple meets for a short time, say, three weeks, and both are full of infatuation but love. They then get married but get separated later after a very short period.

Even though a few couples have been lucky, it is better to have a long courtship of about one year, to enable both understand themselves and find out much about each other.

Thus, courtship or dating gives partners the opportunity to find out if they will be compatible as a couple in marriage.

4. Promiscuity—A partner tries to have a merry-go-round routine simply because sex is now more easily available and affordable through various sophisticated media and can be appropriately priced and paid for in various forms, even with credit cards. The partner keeps getting away with it until the affair is discovered. The innocent partner then takes advantage and files for divorce, without creating any room for discussion, explanation, repentance, and reconciliation.

5. Increasing urbanization and interstate/country movements— Because of this (with due respect to traveling salesmen and other groups of travelers), a person moves out of sight for some time and ignores the partner at home, with little or no consequence, and picks up new relationships, to the detriment of the innocent partner left in the cold. This could go on undetected for years. But once it is discovered, the affair hurts both partners, particularly the innocent partner. The latter starts putting one and one together and recalls all occasions when requests to go out together or pleas to return from tours or trips were turned down because of "pressure of work."

Divorce then becomes a top priority for the aggrieved party.

6. Improved civil rights—Due to these, particularly from declarations by United Nations and similar bodies and the passing of appropriate laws in some countries, people have been asserting their rights and quarrelling in situations which previously would have been tolerated. Women have mostly taken advantage of this liberalization of "human rights" and are eager to break up relationships in order to have and enjoy their "freedom."

7. Inadequate background checks on prospective partners -- Probably because of infatuation and youthful exuberance on the part of partners who fell in love at first sight, proper background checks on claims and past lives of partners were overlooked or poorly conducted. Eventually, when a check or information reveals something adverse (such as the partner having been previously involved in "underground life" such as prostitution, drug dealing, stealing, murder, or something else to be ashamed of), the innocent party tries to walk out of the

relationship. The need for a good background check cannot therefore be overemphasized.

8. Absence of family advice and blessings—Some couples tend to ignore the advice of elderly people and influential family members (who have the benefit of hindsight) when choosing their partners. Your parents may not force you to marry a particular person, but you should at least give them the opportunity to ask pertinent questions that are basic in a relationship and to advise on obvious pitfalls that should be avoided, to ensure success. When couples then have problems, parents are helpless in advising and supporting them. The relationships then roll down the hill. Children these days think they know everything and hardly need advice from the elderly. But they are wrong, as has been proved time and time again.

9. Cultural barriers—Many people seemingly in love tend to ignore the cultural background of their prospective partners.

Partners should reasonably understand the cultural background of the people or group they are marrying into. Spouses can throw a lot of light on this, so that their opposite numbers may know how they will be affected by the culture of their spouses, in life and even after death. Some cultural practices may seem barbaric or antiquated, but to those born into them, the practices are wonderful and spiritually enlivening.

Within the realms of the humanities such as sociology and anthropology, no culture is seen to be superior to the other. Without culture such as a unique, living language, groups of people cannot easily be identified and such people disappear sooner or later and are easily forgotten. They may not even have the opportunity to be declared "endangered species" by UNESCO (United Nations Educational, Scientific and Cultural Organization, an arm of the United Nations), based in Paris, France.

Culture is simply a way of life and encompasses religion, food, greetings, the way houses are built, marriage ceremonies, burial rites or practices, mode of dressing, manner of talking, and even sexual practices and other ways of life. If couples have these at the back of their minds, they will understand themselves better. If not, it is a matter of time before promising marriages fail.

10. Encouragement by divorce lawyers—Because of the heavy fees and costs associated with divorce or separation proceedings, many lawyers find it very lucrative to specialize in this department of law. They charge exorbitant fees, particularly where celebrities are involved. They have even been more innovative by drawing up prenuptial agreements

that cover what each party gets in the event (and a likely one at that) of a separation. In other words, **separation is anticipated even before marriage vows are taken.** What a sad situation! Any wonder then why marriages of many celebrities do not last! The disadvantaged but greedy partner will simply opt out, claim the handsome prize and move on to a life of undeserved luxury thereafter. Lawyers, in my opinion, should first try to reconcile partners and receive God's blessings for doing this. Why should they participate actively and deliberately in dismembering families and loved ones through divorce, except it is inevitable in the case of threatened death or "serious adulterous relationship by the wife?" It appears the latter reason is even supported by the Holy Bible in **Matthew 19:3-12.** Our Lord Jesus Christ said inter alia:

Whoever divorces his wife except for sexual immorality and marries another commits adultery; and whoever marries her who is divorced commits adultery.

You are free to check this out in the Bible.

11. Unwillingness to bear burden or to make changes—Some women do not seem to know that there is a biological clock ticking away against them. Some get married all right, but refuse to be pregnant or decide to postpone pregnancy in favor of their shapes and careers, which they want to keep. Then, in their late thirties or early forties, they suddenly wake up from their deep slumber and remember that they "forgot" to be pregnant or even look for pregnancy in their late twenties or early thirties. This tends to raise their blood pressure, caused by anxiety and fear that they may end up childless, not from lack of fertility but from their own procrastination while flaunting their shapes and beauty. A woman, of course, need not lose her shape because she has had a baby. She can always shape up gradually later. In fact, many women become more beautiful after they have had babies. Many mothers look more shapely than some spinsters do. When, therefore, a male partner wants children early but his wife opts for postponing pregnancies, there may be no meeting point, like two parallel lines that can never meet mathematically. They both go their separate ways.

Some men are also guilty of this procrastination. They remain married to their jobs or careers and forget that they have beautiful wives waiting and wanting to be pregnant. They keep manufacturing excuses until their wives become impatient and frustrated. Then the marriage gradually packs up. However, where partners show understanding and are willing to make compromises, this problem can be worked out or fixed, with both sides coming out happy. You should know your intentions in marriage and communicate these to your prospective partner early to see if there is an acceptable meeting point.

For those divorced or separated who want to marry for the second, third, or fourth time, there is no guarantee whatsoever that this time around they and their partners will be a perfect match or will succeed in remaining in marriage until death comes calling. Multiple marriages can be "hell" for women in particular as name changes are generally involved.

Take a look at this scenario: A woman marries the first husband and becomes Mrs. A. She gets divorced and reverts to her maiden name. She remarries later and becomes Mrs. B and so on until she is tired of going through many husbands or many husbands going through her. Question: How do people recognize that Mrs. A, Mrs. B, and so on are one and the same person? How do the children cope with half-brothers and half-sisters answering different surnames? It is not impossible that these half-relations (who may not know themselves, as apparently they have never lived together under the same roof) may meet and marry each other and before their husband-changing mother knows of it, they may have committed incest in their total innocence. Couples who like to threaten divorce or separation at the slightest provocation should seriously weigh all these problems and others. Many children caught in the crossfire suffer tremendously, physically and emotionally. They are withdrawn, inattentive, and unhappy. They commit violent crimes and suicide, produce children outside wedlock and tend to use drugs, among other problems.

How to go about healing/reconciliation process

What then can be done in respect of these broken-down marriages? Can partners, who have since gone their separate ways like Humpty-Dumpty, ever be brought together again, even by all the king's men and horses?

<u>What to do</u>

The answer to the above question is both "yes" and "no." It depends on so many factors and variables such as:

a) Immediate and remote causes of the divorce
b) Whether children are involved or not.
c) Whether partners have learned their lessons or not and will now be committed
d) The current status of partners (whether they have remarried and have children in the new relationships)
e) Willingness to reach new compromises that will enhance their safety and happiness when they live together again

f) Willing to forgive themselves and forget their immediate past

g) Willingness of a partner to relocate, if necessary in the interest of peace.

This is an area where friends and relations can be of immense help. They should be able to afford the time in shuttling between partners to sound out their opinions and prepare their minds for possible reconciliation. The shuttle diplomacy, like Dr. Henry Kissinger's during the crisis in the Middle East, may take months before any serious discussion begins. It may include taking conditions from one party to the other who may accept or amend them, in the fashion of those trying to enter into a contract with offers, counteroffers, final acceptance, and perhaps with the necessary quid pro quo or consideration. The person who is trying to effect this reconciliation, with the requisite experience, should be able to moderate the terms of settlement if they appear unreasonable or incapable of fulfillment, to enable the "warring parties" come to terms. If you happen to make an acceptable peace (or even for trying), you will surely receive God's blessings as promised in the Lord's Beatitudes during the Sermon on the Mount in Matthew 5:3-11 which goes like this: **"...Blessed are the peacemakers, for they will be called the children of God..."**

Peacemakers (including priests and counselors) can bring parties together in a series of meetings and try to do some trade-offs that will not make either party lose face and be a stumbling block in the reconciliation effort. Separated partners themselves can also take the initiative toward reconciliation by requesting friends or relations to sound out the opinions of their former spouses. Some efforts have been successful while using this approach.

This approach will be easy if both partners have been in touch with each other through occasional visits, letters, and telephone calls. Some separated couples are not unknown to still engage in sexual relations. This situation appears to be a compromise between outright separation and living together under the same roof as husband and wife. It should not be condemned outright on the face of it, so long as third-party interests are not affected, i.e., the men and women have not remarried nor do they have other strong relationships. This kind of relationship can even facilitate an early reconciliation. After all, before God and in the "eyes" of the church and other interested groups, which forbid divorce, they are apparently still married. Professional marriage counselors can also help in bringing back separated partners who should lay all their cards on the table and have a sincere approach to the matter.

In order to have true reconciliation, partners must be factual and willing to come together again. They should properly reflect on those issues that tore them apart in the first place and see if the issues were worth all the trouble they (the partners) have been through. Time may be required to mend a broken heart after so many months or years. But sometimes, time appears to stand still in the minds of divorced couples, which was mentioned by legendary Ray Charles in his very popular and evergreen record **"I can't stop loving you."**

Thus, friends and relations should give a lot of encouragement and support. As is usually the case throughout the period of separation, partners discover that they have not lost sight of themselves. They monitor each other's activities, including any love relationships. This clearly indicates (despite all the initial appeals) that it is not easy to go their separate ways once people have been in love or have been married. While you are in a relationship, you seem to be in prison or a kind of gilded cage. You feel that you will be happier out of it. Outside of the relationship, you want to go back to it because your life seems lonely and empty. No one seems to love you or feel concerned for you.

Human beings seem not to be happy with any position in which they find themselves. They are not happy with their God-given bodies and want to make improvements through plastic surgery, makeup and special treats, which these days, make some people look like masquerade. This, incidentally, leaves them even unhappier and they keep making artificial improvements at a great cost, but to the benefit of plastic surgeons and sellers of cosmetic products.

You generally feel hurt when you hear that your former partner is now in love with someone else. You start to wonder if there is anything that the new person has which you lack. Surely, you have blood running in your veins as well as human feelings. However, some pretend not to have these feelings and tend to "show off" that they are happier in their new relationships. But right inside them, they may not be happy at all.

For partners genuinely interested in true reconciliation, they should be prepared to make *compromises and sacrifices*, particularly where children are involved. **Children themselves, if mature, can play a unifying role** and even force terms on their separated parents to come together, under threat of severing their relationship from them if they do not comply.

Genuine reconciliation is a two-way street involving giving and taking. There will be no winners and no losers but all winners. The man wins, the woman wins, the children win, relations and friends win, and the society wins when reconciliation is successful. You should be ready to bend backwards a little bit, shift grounds, and accommodate your partner. No matter the problem, there is always a solution, one way or another.

People should take a good look at those who have celebrated their tenth, fifteenth, twentieth, fiftieth, or sixtieth wedding anniversaries and find out the secret of their success. You will find the same theme throughout—accommodation, love, sacrifice, truth and faithfulness, among other virtues.

Does anyone want to be one of the divorce statistics?

Your mind will be greatly at rest when you live together with a loved one, rather than employ private detectives to follow your ex-partner around and report back on new dalliances. Employing detectives to follow your erstwhile spouse around seems to suggest that you are still in love. Then, why not take the right steps toward full reconciliation? Is the reluctance due to the fact that "so much water has passed under the bridge," by your own reckoning? Is it not possible that little or no water at all has passed?

There is nothing to be ashamed of if the first step toward reconciliation fails. Not everyone succeeds the first time or even a second time. It should be remembered that where there is a will, there would always be a way. You should therefore keep trying until success is achieved.

Once partners are reconciled, they should never go back to the hurtful, old ways again, because this time around, any minor incident will bring back memories of the earlier divorce or separation, rocking the boat again and perhaps sinking the marriage forever. So, they should be very careful about their utterances and actions. They should show more understanding and love as never before. They should make use of the reinvigorated marriage. There may be little or no time to enjoy the presence of their children, as the latter mature and move out to live on their own.

Reconciliation is like being born again while divorce or separation is like death or emptiness or a void. People are sad when there is a divorce or a separation but are happy when reconciliation or marriage takes place. So, partners should always play up the positive aspects of marriage while playing down the negative aspects.

However, where third party relationships are involved (i.e., where one of the partners has remarried), what should be done by a separated or divorced partner? The answer is not quite as clear cut. If children are involved in the new relationship (i.e., one of the divorcees has children in the new relationship), they should not be thrown out, as they are quite innocent. In this exceptional circumstance, one may as well allow sleeping dogs to lie, i.e., the new relationship should not be rocked because of the children. But if children are not involved and the ex-partners wish to come together again, they should go ahead and get reconciled because before God both are still husband and wife. The third party now disappointed will then learn a bitter lesson in life—not to toy with any previously married person. The ball is now in your court. The first giant step should be taken towards effecting reconciliation. Your life should now change for the better.

Some divorce statistics worldwide
I.
Divorce Rate in the U.S.A. (Annual rate per 1,000 population)

Year/Period	Rate
1960	2.5%
1970	3.1%
1980	5.1%
1990	4.9%
1999	4.1%

II.
Global Divorce Rate (As a percentage of all marriages)

Country	Rate
Russia	65%
Sweden	64%
Finland	56%
Britain	53%
U.S.A	49%
Canada	45%
France	43%
Germany	41%
Israel	26%
Greece	18%
Spain	17%
Italy	12%

(Source: Time Magazine—Sept 25, 2000 page 76)

A notable observation here is that, contrary to privately and popularly held notions, the U.S.A. is not the divorce capital of the world. The "dubious honor" belongs to Russia, Sweden, and Finland, in that order.

The same publication shows that the chance of divorce is highest during the early years—between third and fifth year. Furthermore, in the case of the U.S.A., the rate doubled between early sixties and early eighties, but has been declining since then. The reasons for the decline can, perhaps, be traced to more tolerance on the part of couples, increasing background checks before committing themselves, and overall reluctance of people to get married, preferring instead to remain single and uncommitted and have children under a free atmosphere, devoid of a watching or incompatible spouse.

Some factors which influence divorce

As can be seen above, many factors seem to influence the high rate of divorce:
a) Applicable marriage/divorce laws—liberal or conservative.
b) Traditional views of marriage and ties to in-laws and those around.
c) Spousal independence of each other for income and other needs. The more independent they are, the more the likelihood of divorce.
d) Religion in which divorce is granted/tolerated or denied completely.
e) Lifestyles of couples—drunkenness/drug usage and/or violence.
f) Level of tolerance of faults in a marriage/patience of partners.
g) Age of couples and extent of courtship.
h) Other local factors.

Where easy circumstances or conditions exist or permit, divorce rate tends to be very high, but where those circumstances are absent or difficult, divorce rate tends to be low. Is it any surprise that in developing countries of Africa, Asia, and Latin America, where family ties are still very strong and where some marriages are still arranged in one form or another, the divorce rates are extremely low? Is it any wonder that Italy, a Catholic country, has a low divorce rate? At the extreme end is Russia, where drunkenness and little or no religion during the "high points" of the Communist rule contributed heavily to the high divorce rate there.

Let each couple give their marriage a chance.

Highlights

Divorce and separation are on the increase due to selfish reasons.

Everyone should be concerned and should work to bring the rate down.

Friends, relations, and institutions should effect reconciliation between divorced or separated couples.

No one gains in a divorce. All are losers.

Compromises, sacrifices, and forgiving spirit are necessary in reconciliation.

Genuine reconciliation involves giving and taking, like a two-way street.

Everybody gains when there is reconciliation.

Chapter 15

In Perspective

*"Play well your role in life as envisaged by nature
and you will be happy in the end."*

Happiness through commitment and contentment

Marriage is a beautiful union of man and woman. To have a lasting and happy relationship, a couple should nurture the union and work hard to ensure its success. Nothing good comes easy. Everyone wants to celebrate silver, golden and diamond jubilees of their marriage.

Thus, great material acquisitions do not make marriages or homes. Even though they are good to own, they should not be worshipped. Just like bread, man does not live by them alone, yet he cannot live without some material acquisitions. Partners should be satisfied with whatever they have or can afford and help others to be happy.

It is not enough to be married on paper. Both husband and wife should form a "perfect union" and be almost one in nearly everything they do. By obeying God's and nature's laws, respecting each other, showing love toward each other, reaching compromises and making necessary sacrifices, both husband and wife are sure to succeed. It should be remembered that some lower animals have permanent partners throughout life. If this is so, why should human beings, who are far higher on the social order, not do better? Marriage should not be toyed with if one is not ready for it in all its ramifications. One should play one's role very well and watch the rewards roll in. These include, but are not limited to, happiness, long life, responsible children, good health, and respect within the community.

144

Remember that to err is human, but to forgive is divine. People should learn from the mistakes of others and avoid unpleasant situations. When you fall, you rise and learn not to fall again, while avoiding pitfalls. But when you fall and refuse to rise up or even find out why you fell, you are admitting defeat. This is not what life encompasses. Many inventions or conveniences people enjoy today did not come through after a single attempt. There were series of errors, trials, corrections, and even fatal accidents before the inventions were perfected. So also is marriage, which is still being perfected. It is still a wonder in nature how unlike charges attract each other while like charges repel each other; how a man and a woman who, perhaps, do not know each other very well can decide to live together under the same roof for procreation and other purposes. The spirit of compromise is very strong and should be practised as much as possible if you are to remain happy. Your views and way of life should, as much as possible, blend with your partner's and neighbor's to ensure a happy relationship and happy environment.

For separated couples, the time to act is *now*. It should not be postponed for any reason. There will always be reasons for not doing something if you do not want to. Everything people do has its beneficial and negative effects. If they practise evil, the law of retributive justice (Karma) is waiting to take its toll, in one form or another. It cannot be escaped. The toll could be on anybody --wife, husband, children, grandchildren, or distant relations, but there is no escaping it. **So, try to start fence-mending today.**

Couples who are happily married should continue to cement and nurture their unions, in the same way plants and ideas are nurtured to keep them alive.

People sometimes wonder why some jobs call for married people. The answer is simple. Married people living together have to be tolerant, accommodating, patient, compromising, and responsible in order to stay on together. All these qualities and more are usually brought to bear on jobs where all shades of opinions and characters and people from diverse cultures and backgrounds are seen or dealt with. Thus, if people have remained successfully married, they should reasonably succeed at these jobs. So, remain married and earn a lot of respect.

Reaping the benefits of marriage and love

In their twilight years, a successful husband and his loving wife will reap the fruits of their labor. Thus, according to the Holy Bible, Psalm 128:3-4:

Your wife shall be like a fruitful vine in the very heart of your house, your children like olive plants all around your table. Behold, thus shall the man be blessed who fears the Lord.

Lastly, one should read or listen to St. Paul's Epistle to the Colossians. St. Paul, it is known, was never married. All the same, he was able to offer advice to couples on the need to remain faithful and show love to one another. He was a major force in the spread of the gospel in the early years of Christianity. He advised people, through various writings and visits, on the need to remain married as husbands and wives, with children, in the fear of the Lord. In chapter **3:18-21**, his exhortation is:

Wives, submit to your own husbands, as is fitting in the Lord. Husbands love your wives and do not be bitter towards them. Children, obey your parents in all things, for this is well pleasing to the Lord.

As can be seen, wives are advised to obey their husbands, as they would the Lord. This is a major source of problems today, particularly in the families of celebrities and other highly placed people where some wives find it difficult to obey simple orders and respect their husbands in a manner that befits the latter. On the other hand, some husbands do not love their wives sufficiently, if at all. Loving them means a lot—assuring them always of their happiness and welfare, expressing undying love for them, listening to their problems and concerns and helping to solve them, and generally treating them well, not as trash as some men are accustomed to doing. If men and women would listen to people like St. Paul, there would hardly be any problems in marriage, particularly in the areas of separation and divorce. Life is too short to permit any kind of unhappiness with a partner, friends, or relations. The happier you are, all things remaining equal, the longer you are expected to live. People's selfish and narrow interests always take the center stage when there is a slight problem in a relationship.

For a repentant partner, the mere mention of three words "I am sorry" goes a long way toward healing and softening the heart of an aggrieved partner. Yet many people ignore this approach and prefer a confrontation that is uncalled for. Partners should also remember the advice of our Lord Jesus Christ when He mentioned one of the greatest things to do in order to gain God's favor:

Do unto others as you would want them to do to you.

This equally translates to: "Love thy neighbor as thyself."

From good families, a good village will emerge, then a good city, county or borough and state, and finally a good world. The reverse is equally true. Bad families eventually influence or contribute to the emergence of bad citizens. Whatever happens to a single family—good or bad—will reflect on the entire society or nation. Watch crime statistics from countries where divorce rate is quite high and where other forms of sexual abuse or permissiveness are practised, all in the name of freedom. They have reached epidemic proportions.

So, let everyone put aside selfish interests and play their roles well. You will see a beautiful world emerge.

Highlights
All couples should show genuine love toward their partners.

A marriage should be built on a good foundation, so that partners reap the benefits at old age.

Love your neighbor as yourself.

Chapter 16

Downside of Marriage: Flirtation and Divorce

"Do unto others as you would want them do unto you"

Flirtation/adultery/unfaithfulness

All marriages, after courtship, should actually be made in heaven. But this is wishful thinking as some marriages fail or pack up, even after a few days or before the ink on the dotted line dries up. You then begin to wonder why the couples decided to marry, with all the flamboyance and troubles. A notable celebrity in the USA ended her marriage within fifty five hours in early 2004. You then begin to wonder whether people understand what marriage is all about or not, and if they are in the right frame of mind. If couples courted for a reasonable length of time and loved each other, they should be able to tolerate one another and work out any problems bedeviling their relationship.

Many a time, either the man or woman flirts and even flaunts it before the spouse. Having chosen your partner or spouse, you should try to avoid flirting, as it hurts a relationship, particularly when it is discovered. It is even worse when you are involved with someone far below your social status. If, however, for whatever reason, you decide to flirt (may be it is in your blood), it should be done with a lot of prudence and discreetness in order not to offend your spouse.

Some people are flirts by nature and they invariably continue to enjoy this dangerous game, no matter their marital status. Some do this and keep changing partners as if the latter were dresses or shoes, which have no feelings.

Flirting and incompatibility of partners are probably the greatest reasons cited in divorce proceedings. Unfaithfulness and divorce are also the greatest problems that hurt relationships. While nothing can be done to eliminate these, they can be controlled and significantly reduced, or at least done with some respect so as not to injure the feelings of the spouse. The problem has been with mankind for thousands, if not millions, of years. There is nothing new under the sun, as the saying goes. Some cultures tolerate flirting for both the husband and his wife while others do not tolerate it, particularly for the wife; so it is good for an intending couple to know what can or cannot be tolerated, notwithstanding cultural similarities or differences.

Finding out: signs to look out for

The victim can usually find out if the spouse is cheating or flirting through a number of ways. Nevertheless, these, among others, are not foolproof:

1. Reports from friends, relations, and other sources.
2. Spouse stays out late most of the time or goes out at unusual hours.
3. Unidentified phone calls or strange messages left behind.
4. Going out most of the time without the spouse and traveling alone for prolonged periods.
5. Use of credit cards for suspicious items or a large shortage of cash that cannot be accounted for.
6. Frequent visits to friends or relations who could be providing cover or space for the flirt.
7. Unusual criticisms of spouse: manner of dressing, cooking, etc.
8. Visible tell-tale signs: letters, lipstick stains, strange cologne on body or dress, bringing home strange items not belonging to either spouse. In some cases, flirts have been found with the *underwear* of their lovers. How embarrassing and inexplicable!
9. Showering or washing up after an outing except it has been usual to do so.
10. Picking up an STD from spouse, if victim has not had sex with an outsider.
11. Giving excuses for not having sex with spouse. This is probably a sign that the cheat is tired from his/her outings and may not be able to perform satisfactorily with the spouse at the material time.
12. Purchase of condoms by the male spouse (and in some cases by the female) when he does not normally use them on the partner, and the condoms keep going down in number on a regular basis. Condoms are rarely used for other purposes.

    Some people do admit to their partners that they are into other relationships, but this is generally dangerous, as the victims may react violently. Some victims tolerate this in the hope that the flirts will change and come back home finally. Some do change while others do not.

What a victim should do

What can a victim do? Many things.

Do not rush into conclusion without a thorough investigation, as some signs may be misleading and are mere smoking guns. If you can afford it, hire a private investigator to dig up information discreetly. If you cannot afford one, then be on the lookout for <u>more obvious signs</u> while remaining patient. Do not show any anger or frustration towards your spouse. It obviously hurts if someone who is innocent is wrongly accused. So, be careful. If you prove your suspicions, proceed as enumerated below.

Ask your partner and confront him or her with your suspicions if you know he or she will not be violent in response. If you are proved wrong, then offer unreserved apology with a good or passionate kiss and later treat your spouse to the best sex ever. This is just one way to restore good relationship.

If he or she is likely to be violent, the reaction may have dire consequences such as injury or even death; so invite some trusted friends and relations and confront him or her directly. In the presence of these people, the tendency to be violent will be significantly reduced.

Report to your priest, pastor, rabbi, or imam who may invite him or her for counseling.

Both of you should see a marriage counselor if you still want to stay put in the relationship. This is advisable.

If you do not want to continue with the relationship (and this should be the *last resort*), just move out and talk to a divorce lawyer to commence divorce proceedings. This subject will be touched upon in a subsequent section.

For now, I have some advice for those who cannot stop flirting and also wish to keep their marriage. It is like enjoying the best of both worlds, just like eating your cake and having it.

This sounds paradoxical but it can work out if you have a loving and forgiving partner who is willing to look the other way, and you manage to keep the affair away from home. The victim should remember that good partners have apparently dried up out there and should make do with what is available. It is a hard choice, like being between Scylla and Charybdis.

Advice for flirting partners***

Before you start flirting, ask yourself so many times what you stand to gain or lose. Be factual. Lay all the facts on the table. Thereafter, if you still have the mind to go ahead with all the risks, then proceed as follows:

Do not go out and stay beyond one or two hours without your partner or spouse's knowledge.

Do not leave any tell-tale signs.

Do not give your home telephone number to your friend, or write any letters for fear of being exposed later, particularly in societies where secrets are not easily kept and where people like to make money out of a scandalous situation by revealing intimate secrets in books, television, Internet, and other information media. You should therefore ensure that your mistress or sugar daddy is the type who will not spill the beans on television or in the press and embarrass you and your spouse. Unfortunately, embarrassing situations are now usually the order of the day. So, you cannot be too careful about this. You are warned!

Tell him or her that you are well married and that you love your spouse. If need be, and in particular if you are a celebrity, sign an agreement in advance to cover all possible sexual acts, spelling out that each participant must not withdraw from a sexual act before its completion and without the express permission of the other participant and that no charges of rape must ever be brought before the courts, nor must the sexual acts or liaison ever be mentioned to the press or other news media or individuals. This is a tall order, but experience is the best teacher. Find out what happened to some celebrities and learn a valuable lesson and be free from embarrassment. If you do not cover your grounds very well, then you have yourself only to blame by being caught pants down.

Do not make promises that you cannot keep or that can put you in trouble.

Do not share secrets with friends, as the latter may betray you or let you down. Once you tell a friend, the friend will tell his friend and so on, ad infinitum. Friends have been known to betray friends not only in sex matters but also in politics and other spheres of life. Remember Julius Caesar telling Brutus: "Et tu Brute?" as he was being stabbed to death. So, be careful.

Explain to your date that you do not want children outside marriage and pray that this understanding is kept.

Call your home and promise to be back soon. In this connection, decide how long you can spend away from home without raising any suspicions.

Give good reasons for staying extra hours: broken-down car, shopping, visiting a sick friend or relation who is unknown to your spouse (otherwise he or she may call to find out if you were there), staying late at work to finish a job, visiting an official client, heavy traffic or accident at rush hour, etc.

Ask yourself periodically if your actions are good and what you are gaining, and the likely consequences when you are eventually caught, such as divorce from your spouse, public humiliation, in some cultures before your children and relations. The overall cost may be too high to be easily forgotten in one's lifetime. Flirting, like everything else we do or engage in, is habitual. It takes a hard resolve to stop a bad habit such as smoking, drinking, and being on drugs. Do not take your partner for granted, as a day of reckoning may be at the corner. Discipline yourself and live within expectations. Show good example.

Do not admit to your spouse that you are flirting except if you want to end your marriage. Admitting it means that you do not love your spouse sufficiently and that you do not have any regards for him or her. This hurts.

If you are caught, do not own up. Give excuses for what happened except if you are caught pants down, in which case you should apologize and promise to stop your waywardness. You should even do more to regain the confidence of your spouse.

Always shower or wash up when you get home or at the meeting point, to reduce chances of passing STDs to your innocent spouse.

Always use condom, except you can vouch that your partner is in the clear. Remember that your friend could have multiple partners, so you cannot really vouch for anyone. Be prudent and take precaution.

As soon as your spouse discovers your intimate friend, you must drop him or her to avoid unnecessary jealousy and possible danger to life arising from this.

As far as possible, do not pick a friend from the vicinity where you live or work. It is too close for comfort. Go far away where chances of being discovered are quite minimal.

If you send or buy a gift, make sure that your name is not indicated therein in any way. Even using nicknames is considered risky. Find a suitable code to use and change this regularly, like a **PIN** number. This makes discovery extremely difficult.

If you have a date and your spouse insists on going out with you, this is okay. Drive to a friend's house, a club, a mechanic's shop, or elsewhere and stay as long as possible, to his or her discomfort. Then try reaching your date with your cell phone from a safe spot such as the restroom to cancel the appointment.

Never leave any items of clothing, pictures, or documents bearing your names in a friend's house, except in an official capacity.

As far as possible, avoid being seen together with your intimate friend. Arrange to go to your rendezvous separately, except you are out of the country or immediate vicinity of your home or office and you feel it is safe to be together.

If it comes to choosing between your spouse and your friend, you are advised to choose your spouse for various reasons. Your spouse must always stand out. Your friend or date took a known risk and was aware you were married right from the beginning.

Keep your affairs away from your children, particularly those under eighteen.

When you want to break off a relationship, ensure you do it in a nice way, possibly with a parting present, so as to reduce the chances of your friend harboring ill feelings and the notion of having been used. Avoid breaking off and coming back again and again.

Watch what you eat or drink when you are together to avoid being harmed. It is always prudent to finish your food or drink before leaving the scene, even to go to the restroom.

Do not expose or condemn your spouse before your friend by saying ugly things or telling lies in order to gain some favors. Spouses are known to be conservative about sex and sexual positions, but do not condemn him or her. You can experiment your fantasies with your friend.

Quit if it becomes necessary and confess to your spouse before the matter becomes messy. Do not give a detailed, graphic account, even if requested by your spouse, as this is bound to be very hurtful. Pretend that you were out of your mind when you did certain things. In some countries, voodoo may be used to cause problems in an erstwhile beautiful relationship.

Once you observe these simple and common sense rules, you may not be caught and you may end up eating your cake and having it. But you should also ask yourself what you gained from all this flirting. No doubt, nothing, absolutely nothing in the end!

However, it must be emphasized again that the best way to have a happy relationship, from dating or courtship stage to marriage, is to remain faithful to your friend, mate or spouse. Try it. It works.

Steps to take in a divorce***

Sometimes divorce is inevitable in a previously happy relationship, for various reasons. Nobody prays for this. But when it seems imminent, a spouse should do his or her homework properly before proceeding with the divorce.

Some useful points may be made for the guidance of a spouse if he or she is the underdog and expects to obtain the best settlement:

Make a good estimate of your spouse's income, now and in future.

Know what position he holds in an establishment and number of years he or she has been there.

Obtain copies of all relevant documents, bank/credit card statements, landed properties (developed or undeveloped), cars, boats, airplanes, etc.

Document your lifestyle when you were together: the kind of lifestyle you both enjoyed including traveling, etc.

Remember the number of children you have, their schools and lifestyle and what it costs to maintain them including medical and nanny expenses, etc.

Estimate what it will cost to eat and drink monthly and pay bills, including buying dresses, shoes, etc.

Estimate your legal fees and counseling costs.

Ensure you watch your safety always as an unscrupulous spouse could plan evil against you at this time, to avoid paying alimony and/or child support.

Other useful information, as considered necessary.

Armed with this information, you should see a good divorce lawyer to take it up from there. He will then arrange to see your spouse's lawyer. Anything you remember should be communicated to your lawyer. You never can say what is important in a divorce case. When it comes to final settlement, let your mind guide you. Be honest. Thus, you should neither be greedy nor timid about the monetary compensation.

A bad or less satisfying private settlement is preferable to going to court to face questioning and exposure of your life style from your spouse's lawyer.

So, know at what point to yield.

As has been said previously, divorce is nasty and should be avoided at all costs, except there is a real threat or danger to one's life, and the marriage is definitely beyond redemption.

Highlights

Flirting/unfaithfulness, along with health implications, causes the breakup of couples and families and should be avoided at all costs.

If you suspect your spouse is flirting, look out for obvious signs but do not rush into wild conclusions and confrontation about it without being one hundred percent certain. Be a little bit more patient and observant.

Try to resolve the problem through friends and other people.

When it becomes necessary to go separate ways, be sure to obtain the advice of a good lawyer, but weigh the consequences of divorce.

Chapter 17

ABC of Successful Courtship and Marriage

"As you make your bed so shall you lie"

Mnemonic Presentation: A-Z

These letters of the English alphabet are mnemonic—aiding or designed to aid the memory—in love matters. Going through them and practising them will help a great deal in successfully handling one's partner and other relationship matters. Here goes:

A — Affection unlimited for each other. Each spouse is the other's "Alter Ego" (other person or better half).

B — Balanced lifestyle. Belief in success.

C — Caring for each other and children. Compromise and Courtship—a must. Consideration for each other's feelings.

D -- Dependence on each other. Desire for each other. Divorce is an anathema and is not in the marriage dictionary.

E — Endeavoring to please. Enthusiasm for each other's job or decent lifestyle. Endeared to each other.

F — Faithfulness to each other. Fondness for each other. Faith in success and in life. Forgiveness from the heart. Forging ahead with life.

G — Godliness in all activities. Gossips to be shunned. Goodness to all. Gentility towards each other.

H — Happiness at all times. Home to replace a house. Hope for the best at all times.

154

I — Interacting with in-laws and friends. Be an Instrument of peace.

J — Joined forever in wedlock. "What God has joined together, let no man put asunder."

K — Knowing each other well—both weaknesses and strengths.

L — Love unlimited for each other. Lifelong relationship. Loyalty to each other.

M — Making up to each other in difficult situations and when one offends the spouse.

N — Nurturing the relationship from time to time. Never going to bed with a heavy heart. Never Nagging. Never forgetting to forgive.

O — Observing changes in the lifestyle of a partner and carefully handling undesirable developments, with outsiders knowing very little or nothing about any problems.

P — Patience is a virtue and is rewarding. It should be practised, as one needs it throughout one's life. Politeness always.

Q — Quit grumbling and lay problems on the table. "Quid pro quo" (something for something) to be practised. Quiet approach to settlement of quarrels and misunderstandings.

R — Respect for each other's views and practising self-respect and self-restraint. Reaching out to the less fortunate.

S — Seducing each other periodically. Separation is not in the marriage dictionary

T — Teasing each other's sensual parts of the body. Touching each other regularly—holding, kissing, and making eye contact. Keep talking. Teaching children to master the world. Tolerating each other.

U — Uniting all family members—immediate and remote. Having a united mind at all times. Understanding all issues and showing this at all times.

V — Vicissitudes of life to be remembered always. There are usually ups and downs, and appropriate adjustments should be made accordingly.

W — Weathering all storms that try to rock a marriage. The journey through life and marriage is rough and stormy but highly rewarding.

X — X-raying all actions and ensuring fairness to partner and family. Xeroxing all good actions for posterity.

Y — Yielding to one's mate on nonsensitive issues rather than arguing endlessly. Admitting it when one is wrong.

Z — Zero in on every opportunity to improve your love life. Zygotes of husband and wife—children—should never be used to attack each other; otherwise a partner loses respect before the children. Zeal to succeed must be present at all times

Glossary

1. **"Gordian Knot"**—Chapter 1:
This was an intricate knot tied by **Gordius**, an ancient Phrygian king in Asia Minor (most of today's Turkey). The knot was made in such a way that it was incapable of being untied except by a future ruler of Asia Minor. For a long time, it remained untied, no matter how many times people tried, until Alexander the Great (the war general and conqueror) cut through it with his sword. He thus untied the Gordian knot.

The expression "untying the Gordian knot" is now used figuratively to refer to a difficulty that can be overcome only by the application of bold and unusual measures or when someone accomplishes a seemingly impossible or difficult task.

2. **"To cross the Rubicon"**—Chapter 1:
The Rubicon is a river in Italy separating Caesar's former province of Gaul (today's France) from Italy. By crossing it, Gaius Julius Caesar (Roman general, statesman and dictator) committed himself to war with Pompey (Roman general and statesman and a member of the first Triumvirate).

It is now used to show commitment to something to which there is no turning back, or overcoming a difficult task; *to take a final, irrevocable step.* When Gaius Julius Caesar crossed the river at the head of his army to march on Rome in 49 B.C., he began the civil war with Pompey the Great. Another way to put this is: "The die is cast" (In Latin: Jacta est alea). This statement was also ascribed to Julius Caesar, while trying to cross the Rubicon as stated above.

3. **"Minotaur"**—Chapter 1:
This was a monster in Greek mythology. It was half man and half bull and was confined in an elaborate maze—the Labyrinth in Crete—where it was annually fed human flesh until it was killed by Theseus, the chief hero of Attica, an ancient Greek kingdom that had Athens as its capital.

The labyrinth was an intricate structure or enclosure having a series of winding passages, which were hard to follow without losing one's way. Daedalus built such a structure for King Minos of Crete to house the Minotaur. The labyrinth is now used, figuratively, to refer to a complicated or perplexing arrangement or course of affairs.

4. **"Adonis"**—Chapter 2:
In Greek mythology, this is a youth beloved by Venus for his handsomeness. It is now usually used to refer to a very handsome and well sculptured man.

5. **"Aphrodite"**—Chapter 2:

In Greek mythology, this is the goddess of love and beauty. It is used to refer to a very beautiful or attractive woman.

6. **"Venus"**—Chapter 2:
In Roman mythology, this is the goddess of love and beauty. It is now used to refer to a very beautiful woman.

7. **"Esto Vir"**—Chapter 2:
Latin for "Be a man." A man takes decisions and sticks to them. His word should be his bond. He would rather face the consequences of his actions than hide or run away when the consequences are unpleasant. This is what being a man means.

8. **"Kola-nuts"**—Chapter 4:
These are two-, three-, four-, or five-lobed nuts in a pod, which is grown as a cash crop in the tropics, particularly in countries of West Africa and Latin America, particularly Brazil. They are neither bitter nor sweet, but are used extensively in ceremonies and in welcoming guests in West Africa. They can also be taken privately by those who like to chew something. They contain some caffeine and so act as a stimulant when chewed. Just as an American or European offers tea or coffee or chocolate when he has a visitor, an African (whose area produces and values these nuts), after the usual greetings/pleasantries, usually offers kola-nuts as the beginning point of meetings, entertainment, and ceremonies, praying for the good things of life while breaking the nuts. He usually apologizes to his guests if there are no kola-nuts or if it is far late into the night for an entertainment. Responsibility for breaking the nuts in the traditional way falls either on the oldest man, or, in some cultures, on the youngest. There are reasons for this approach. The oldest man is usually seen as the wisest and most experienced in life and therefore most qualified to break kola-nuts and pray for others.

Then, those present are served the blessed kola-nuts in descending age order. You may not believe it that many a time this simple distribution of kola-nuts causes quarrels among participants if a younger person is served before a more elderly person. It is difficult for people outside the culture to understand this, but people involved enjoy all the fun and acrimony.

In the case of the youngest person who is asked to break kola-nuts, this is usually taken to mean innocence, as the young man is unlikely to harbor ill feelings toward those present and may not therefore think of poisoning anyone through kola-nuts. Women are generally never involved with breaking kola-nuts, but they partake of it all and enjoy all the blessings and fun that go with breaking and serving the nuts to those present. There may be slight variations here and there in the breaking and serving of kola-nuts, according to the culture of the participants, and where there is a gathering of people from various cultural backgrounds. Sometimes, during a gathering of people from diverse backgrounds, the man who breaks kola-nuts jokes that the gods do not understand any language other than one of the languages in the area where kola-nuts are grown and revered. Prayers are thus said in one of the local languages.

9. **"Dowry"**—Chapter 4:

This is a payment, sometimes token or substantial, made by a man to the family of the girl he intends to marry. It may include material things such as clothes, jewelry, sewing machines, kitchen utensils, etc., for presentation to the bride's mother. In a way, this is a form of compensation to the girl's family for helping raise the girl to a marriageable state. Since a lot of resources and time are used in bringing up a girl, parents expect to be compensated, up to a point, for now giving away their daughter in marriage in which she is supposed to contribute adequately to the well being of her husband. However, in some parts of the world (notably India and some parts of the Far East), it is the girl's family that pays dowry to the bridegroom's family. The reason for this is not quite clear, but it may have to do with the ancient belief that since girls are a "burden" on their parents, whosoever takes that burden off their heads should be "compensated."

In some African cultures, if a wife is divorced, her family is expected to fully repay the dowry price to the ex-husband's family whenever she remarries; otherwise any children born before the dowry is repaid belong to her former husband and will bear his name. There are variations of this customary practice here and there.

10. **"DNA"**—Chapter 6: **Deoxyribo Nucleic Acid (The building blocks of life)**

This refers to any of various nucleic acids that are usually the molecular basis of heredity and are localized especially in cell nuclei. They carry genetic information in the cell and are capable of self replication. Samples for the DNA testing can be picked from most parts of the human body, particularly fluids such as blood and saliva. For the layman's understanding, DNA is like human fingerprint, which is unique to each human being. Analysis of DNA helps law enforcement officers to determine the presence or absence of a person at a crime scene, and thus has helped free many innocent prisoners as well as put many criminals behind bar. Unfortunately, many innocent victims had apparently been executed before this technology was perfected in its present form.

11. **"The Trojan War"**—Chapter 7:

Homer in the Iliad reported this war between Sparta and Troy, both in ancient Greece, many centuries before Jesus Christ was born. The central figure was **Helen**, the wife of Menelaos, who was king of Sparta. Paris, the Trojan Prince, seized her for her exquisite beauty because a goddess had promised him the most beautiful woman alive. Helen happened to be that woman but was abducted by Paris when he went to see Menelaos. The king of Sparta, Helen's husband, could not bear this. So, he invited his brother, King Agamemnon of Mycene, to help him bring back his beautiful wife from Troy.

The expedition or war lasted about ten years until Troy was captured. Hector, the Trojan hero, was killed by Achilles, the Spartan hero, who himself was later killed in battle by Paris who threw an arrow in Achilles' right heel, the only vulnerable spot on his body.

The Iliad, however, recounts only a part of so many events in the war which was fought also because of quarrels among the gods and on account of occasions of betrayal among mortals or humans. Today, "Achilles' heel" is used figuratively to mean a vulnerable or susceptible spot or weakness in any action or undertaking.

12. **"Pandora's Box"**—Chapter 8:

In Greek mythology, Pandora was the first mortal sent by Zeus (supreme deity of the ancient Greeks) with a box into the world. Out of curiosity, she opened the box and let loose all the evils that troubled humans. She was sent by Zeus as a punishment to mankind for the theft of fire by Prometheus. The latter, a titan, had taught mankind the use of fire, which he had stolen from heaven. He was subsequently punished by Zeus, by being chained to a rock where a vulture came each day to eat away his liver, which was made whole again each night. A later version of this mythology suggests that Pandora allowed all human blessings to escape and be lost, leaving only hope.

"Pandora's box" is now used figuratively to refer to a situation in which hurtful or incriminating information or something that was previously unknown is now disclosed and hurts or injures one's feelings.

13. **"IVF"**—Chapter 9:

In vitro fertilization, as explained in the text, generally gave hope to some women who could not conceive naturally. It allowed a lot of ethical questions to be raised, and challenged people's morals. The egg donor, for instance, need not be the carrier of the fetus. Many people could also claim to be the rightful owners of the child in an IVF dispute: the sperm donor, the egg donor, the carrier of the fetus, and the man and woman who have agreed to raise the child. As can be seen, all seem to have a rightful claim. This is where the law must come in fast and ensure there will never be any confusion or conflicting claims in an IVF birth scenario.

14. **"Hippocratic oath"**—Chapter 9:

This is the oath usually received by qualifying medical doctors, which sets forth an ethical code for all doctors. This oath was attributed to Hippocrates, a Greek physician, who lived about 460-377 B.C. He is now usually called the Father of Medicine.

15. **"Spartan Life"**—Chapter 12:

In ancient Greece, Sparta and Athens were strong and rival cities or "city states." While Athenians were easy-going and not disciplined in life, the Spartans were their opposite, disciplining themselves in all spheres of life, particularly in military matters. This aided their various conquests. With time, "Spartan life" came to be used to refer to living by austerity, simplicity, discipline, self-denial, and bravery.

16. **"Pyrrhic Victory"**—Chapter 12:

King Pyrrhus of Epirus in ancient Greece went to war with the Romans at Asculum about 279 B.C. In those days, kings were usually required to lead their armies into battle. Once they were killed, their troops surrendered. In this case, even though he sustained heavy losses of men and materials, he won. However, this was a costly victory.

This expression is now used to refer to a victory won or gained at a ruinous loss or great cost or not worth celebrating.

17. "Animal Cloning"—Chapter 14:

A clone, or genetic duplicate, is created by replacing the nucleus of a female egg cell with the nucleus from the cell of a donor or another person. Then the doctored egg cell is treated with chemicals and subjected to electric charges until it begins dividing into an embryo, just as in normal cell division. Eventually, a female host (another female) carries the embryo in her womb to full term and gives birth to a genetic duplicate of the donor, a human clone. Thus, there is no difference between the original donor and the clone—from head to toe. With the spectacular success of Dolly, the Scottish sheep, human cloning may not be far away as there will be doctors and scientists to experiment with nature. Rich and famous people may, one day, want to clone themselves.

18. "Between Scylla and Charybdis"—Chapter 16

Scylla is a dangerous rock on the Italian side of the Straits of Messina, opposite Charybdis, which are whirlpools off the coast of Sicily, near Italy. Ships or boats had to contend with both and faced a great peril when approaching these natural obstacles.

It is an expression used to indicate two difficulties or perils facing someone, such that neither can be avoided without risking the other. Thus, when one avoids one danger, one runs into the other. One cannot avoid both.

Selected Bibliography

Beck, Aaron T. <u>Love Is Never Enough</u>
Berman, C. <u>Adult Children Of Divorce</u>
Clifford, Notarius and Markman Howard <u>We Can Work It Out</u>
Gray, John <u>Men Are From Mars, Women Are From Venus</u>
Fisher, Helen E. <u>Anatomy of Love – The Natural History of Monogamy</u>
Hendrix, H. <u>Getting the Love You Want: A Guide for Couples</u>
Lederer, W.J. and D. Jackson <u>The Mirages of Marriage</u>
Medved, D. <u>The Case Against Divorce</u>
Stuart, R. <u>Helping Couples Change</u>
Tanenbaum, J. <u>Male and Female Realities: Understanding the Opposite Sex</u>
Weiner-Davis, Michele <u>Divorce Busting – A Step-by-step Approach to Making Your Marriage Loving Again</u>
Weitzman, L. J. <u>The Divorce Revolution</u>

There are many other books on courtship, marriage, divorce, and other matters relating to sex, men, and women (and lower animals) that can be consulted, if you are interested in further reading, research, and analysis.

COURTSHIP AND MARRIAGE "FLOW CHART"

<u>PHASES</u>

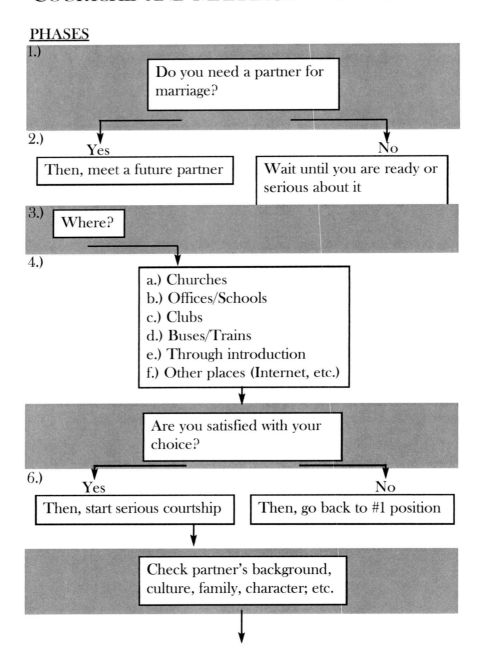

1.)

Do you need a partner for marriage?

2.)

Yes

Then, meet a future partner

No

Wait until you are ready or serious about it

3.)

Where?

4.)

a.) Churches
b.) Offices/Schools
c.) Clubs
d.) Buses/Trains
e.) Through introduction
f.) Other places (Internet, etc.)

Are you satisfied with your choice?

6.)

Yes

Then, start serious courtship

No

Then, go back to #1 position

Check partner's background, culture, family, character; etc.

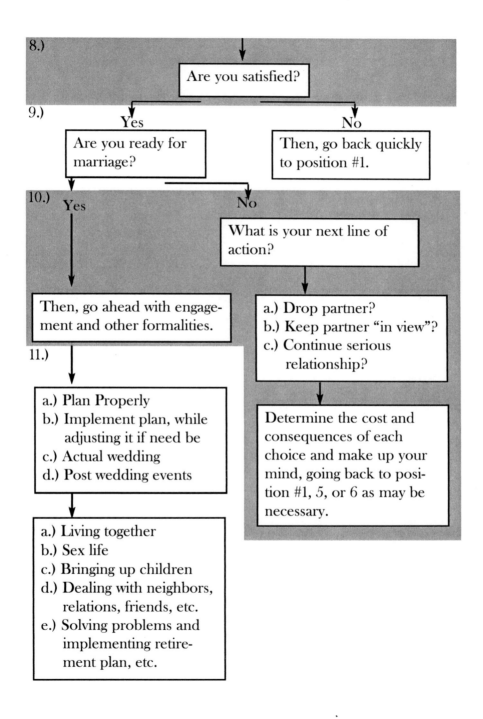

8.) Are you satisfied?

9.)

Yes — Are you ready for marriage?

No — Then, go back quickly to position #1.

10.)

Yes

No — What is your next line of action?

Then, go ahead with engagement and other formalities.

a.) Drop partner?
b.) Keep partner "in view"?
c.) Continue serious relationship?

11.)

a.) Plan Properly
b.) Implement plan, while adjusting it if need be
c.) Actual wedding
d.) Post wedding events

Determine the cost and consequences of each choice and make up your mind, going back to position #1, 5, or 6 as may be necessary.

a.) Living together
b.) Sex life
c.) Bringing up children
d.) Dealing with neighbors, relations, friends, etc.
e.) Solving problems and implementing retirement plan, etc.

About The Author

Albert Chukwudifu Onochie hails from Illah, Delta State of Nigeria, in West Africa. Born in May 1942, he spent his early school years at O.M.S. Abudu (near Benin City), St. Paul's Catholic School Issele-Uku and Catholic School Ubulu-Okiti before completing his elementary school education at St. John's Catholic School, Illah, in December 1955.

He then proceeded to Immaculate Conception College, Benin City where he successfully completed his secondary (high) school education in December 1960.

He taught briefly at the Catholic Junior Seminary, Oke-Are, Ibadan. Thereafter, he worked at Barclays Bank D.C.O. Ibadan (now Union Bank of Nigeria PLC) from April 1961 to September 1964. While there, he obtained the Institute of Bankers Diploma, London (A.I.B.), before resigning in September 1964 to pursue accounting studies at the University of Nigeria, Nsukka. The university was set up in 1960 with the assistance of Michigan State University, East Lansing, Michigan, USA. However, because he was in the war zone at the time (Eastern part of Nigeria, later called Biafra by the secessionists), his studies were interrupted in 1967 by the three-year Nigerian civil war. It ended officially in January 1970 with the federal government's declaration of "No victor, no vanquished," in a bid to reunite the country after the fratricidal and unnecessary war. In its urge to further bring the country together again after the civil war, the federal government introduced on paper three R's as a part of its policy: Reconciliation, Reconstruction, and Rehabilitation. To this day, neither much has been done in those areas adversely affected by the war (the war zone) by way of reconstruction of major infrastructure such as roads, and appointment to major positions of authority in federal government jobs and the military/police force, nor has any serious attempt been made to finally dispose of the outstanding and thorny issue of "abandoned properties" in favor of original owners of those properties. It is a wonder how people can be said to have abandoned their properties in the country they rightfully belong to. This is a part of the anomalies that must be righted if the country must move forward, remain strong and united. To date, only lip service has mostly been paid to the three R's.

After graduating from the University in June 1971 with two academic prizes (faculty and department), he worked with Mobil Oil Nigeria PLC, Nigerian Bank for Commerce and Industry, Volkswagen of Nigeria Ltd., and Bertson Business Corporation Ltd., all based in Lagos. He held top management positions in the last three corporations.

He is a professionally qualified accountant and belongs to a number of professional, civil rights and social bodies including The Chartered Association of Certified Accountants, London; The Chartered Institute of Bankers, London; and The Institute of Chartered Accountants of Nigeria, Lagos. He is also a fellow of The Economic Development Institute (an arm of the World Bank), Washington, D.C., having attended a three-month course in Agricultural Projects Financing in 1976.

A social, civil rights, and political activist, he has traveled (in private and official capacities) to many parts of the world including England, Germany, Italy, France, Switzerland, The Netherlands, Sweden, Austria, India, Cote d'Ivoire, Republic of Benin, Dahomey, United Arab Emirates, and the USA where he has been residing with his family since 1996.

His hobbies include reading, writing, watching documentary films, playing table tennis, and swimming.

He is happily married with five lovely children.

For Comments/Notes